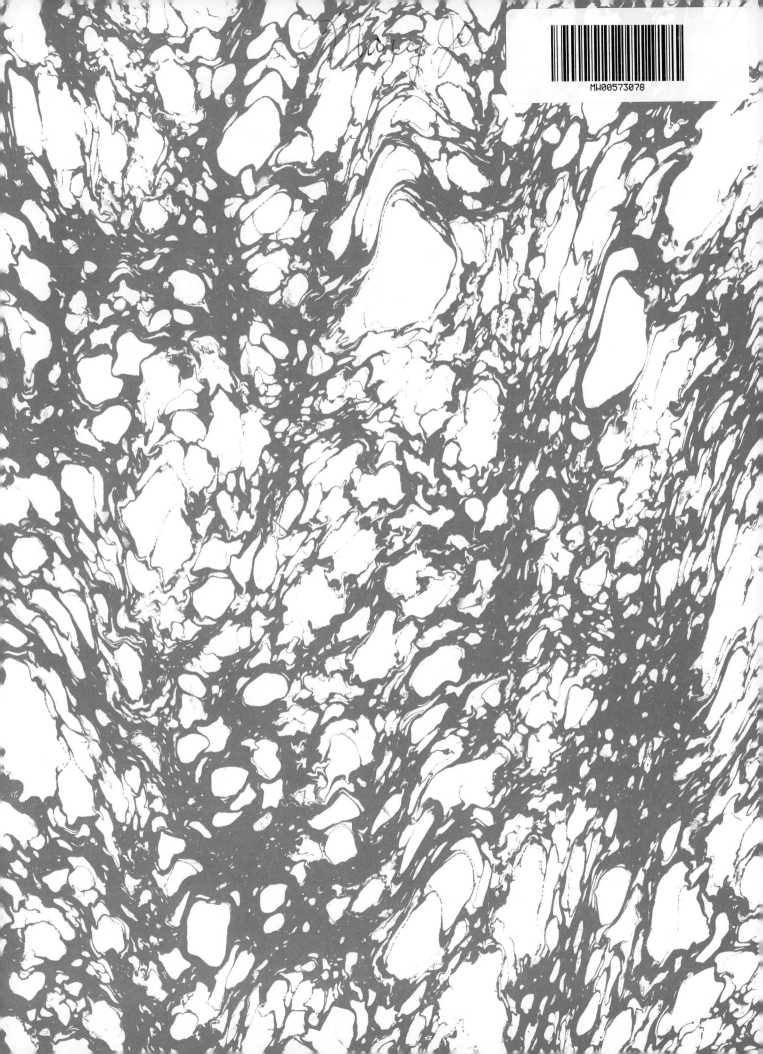

Mary Jo Baumberger
Book Store

Mary Jo Baumberger
Book Store

SIMPLY ITALIAN

MORE THAN 60 QUICK AND EASY RECIPES FROM ITALY

◆◆◆

SIMPLY ITALIAN

MORE THAN 60 QUICK AND EASY RECIPES FROM ITALY

GINA PULICIANO

LONGMEADOW
PRESS

ACKNOWLEDGMENTS

Valuable assistance was provided by the following individuals and organizations: Judi Adams and Margie Martin at the Wheat Foods Council; Alison Athens at the Peanut Advisory Board; Mrs. Julia Cruise at the Italian Trade Commission; Kay Engelhardt at the American Egg Board; Margie Frate and Anita Keeler at Caryl Saunders Associates for the Fresh Garlic Association; Mary Jo Hogue at the USA Rice Council; Emily Holt and Clare Vanderbeck at the National Fisheries Institute; Anita Hudson at the Michigan Asparagus Advisory Board; the Italian Institute for Foreign Trade/ I.C.E.; Robin Kline and Anne Rehnstrom at the National Pork Producers Council; Ming Louie at Ming Photography; Drake McCarthy at Diamond Wine Merchants in Emeryville, CA; Molly Machamer at United Fresh Fruit and Vegetable Association; Gail Rolka; Priscilla Root at the American Lamb Council; Janet Stern at the National Live Stock and Meat Board; Dot Tringali of Newman, Saylor & Gregory for the National Broiler Council.

Published by Longmeadow Press, 201 High Ridge Road, Stamford, CT 06904. All rights reserved. No part of this book may be reproduced or utilized in any form or by any means, electronic or mechanical, including photocopying, recording or by any information storage and retrieval system, without permission in writing from the Publisher.

Cover and interior design by
  Tom Debolski
Edited by Lynne Piade
Food Consultant: Meesha Halm
Contributing Writer: Bill Yenne

ISBN: 0-681-41736-6

Printed in Hong Kong

First Longmeadow Press Edition 1993

0 9 8 7 6 5 4 3 2 1

CONTENTS

INTRODUCTION
6

THE BASICS
8

APPETIZERS
10

SOUPS
16

PIZZA, CALZONE, AND BREADS
20

PASTA, RICE, AND POLENTA
24

SEAFOOD
34

MEATS AND POULTRY
38

VEGETABLES
48

SALADS
52

SWEETS
54

APPENDICES
60

INDEX
64

FOUR SEASONAL MENUS

SPRING
LAMB CHOPS ROMANA *page 44*
BAKED ASPARAGUS *page 51*
LEMON ICE *page 58*
CHIANTI *page 61*

SUMMER
ANTIPASTO PLATTER *page 10*
PIZZA MARGHERITA *page 23*
CALAMARI FESTIVAL STYLE *page 37*
CHOCOLATE GELATO *page 59*
SOAVE *page 61*

FALL
BRUSCHETTA *page 14*
SPAGHETTI ALLA CARBONARA *page 26*
PORK STEW PIEDMONTESE *page 46*
TIRAMI SU *page 59*
BAROLO *page 61*

WINTER
BAGNA CAUDA *page 13*
OSSO BUCO *page 41*
RISOTTO ALLA MILANESE *page 33*
HAZELNUT BISCOTTI *page 55*
BARBARESCO *page 61*

INTRODUCTION

Buon appetito!

Italy is a wonderful world of fabulous vistas, celebrated cities and magnificent countrysides. It is an ancient place with an art and culture of breathtaking depth and richness, yet it is a relatively new nation of splendid diversity and a remarkable people who seem as fresh as the morning dew on the olive trees of Tuscany or the pines of Rome.

Italy is also home to an extraordinary cuisine which has inspired the imagination of chefs and food-lovers throughout the world.

By the end of the sixteenth century, as the Renaissance was changing the course of the world's cultural history, Italian cuisine had reached the level of an art form and had begun to change the course of the world's culinary history. The art and learning that defined the Renaissance was born in Italy and in turn spread to Europe and the world. So too did Italian cuisine become the wellspring from which would evolve all the other great European culinary traditions.

The pivotal moment came in 1533, when Catherine di Medici traveled from Florence to France to become the wife of Henri II. She brought with her the cooks, the pastry chefs, the ingredients and the recipes that would change the face of French and continental cuisine forever.

Italian cuisine in the form that we've come to know and love, has its roots in the culinary traditions of Imperial Rome. Roman cooking had in turn grown out of ancient regional cuisines of the central Mediterranean, such as those of the Greeks and Etruscans. As the Roman Empire reached the apogee of its power, its culinary arts were colored by influences—from Africa to England, from Spain to Persia—that were encountered in the process of empire-building. In the course of this evolution, the Roman cuisine became increasingly sophisticated, witnessing the development of a dozen types of cheeses and the invention of cheesecake.

By the time of Christ, Rome was the major world power and its markets teemed with fruits, vegetables, spices, meats, and other delights from the far-flung reaches of the Empire as well as from the Italian peninsula. From this grew the world's first great international cuisine. However, as the Empire crumbled, the cuisine of the newly-fragmented city-states became simpler and more diverisfied. Italian cooks came to depend on the agricultural goods at hand and their fresh, healthy cuisine created a standard that has survived virtually unchanged to this day.

The beginnings of a truly Italian culture and cuisine had begun to emerge in the twelfth century, and with this came a readoption of many of the old Roman customs, such as multiple course meals. Spices that had fallen into disuse came back into favor, and many of the exotic fruits and foodstuffs of the Middle East were reintroduced by Crusaders returning from those regions that had been part of the Roman Empire a millennium before. Coffee first made its way to Europe by way of Italy.

By this time, pasta had begun to emerge—in many of today's familiar forms—as a staple of Italian cooking. It has been said that pasta first was introduced to Italy when Marco Polo returned from China at the end of the thirteenth century, but in fact, books including pasta recipes had been published before he left. By the fifteenth century large commercial-scale pasta factories were operating in Naples.

Italian cuisine evolved into a true art form while the rest of Europe was still in the Dark Ages. Even before Catherine di Medici introduced Italian cooking to France, there were cooking schools in Florence and Venice. In fact the Italians had béchamel—a creamy white sauce made from butter, flour, milk, seasoned with salt, pepper, and nutmeg—before the French. Cortez introduced tomatoes into Spain from Mexico in 1554, but it was the Italians who cultured them and transformed them from tiny yellow fruits—pomo d'oro or golden apples—into the juicy red keystone ingredient in so many favorite Italian sauces.

Italy as a single unified nation did not emerge until the middle of the nineteenth century, so for the four centuries beginning with the dawn of the Renaissance, Italy was an amalgam of independent, often antagonistic, city-states. It was this condition that led to the development of many of the distinctive regional dishes that today are the vivid

An open-air vegetable market in Florence

threads that form the tapestry of Italian cuisine. These range from the wild game of the north, to the delicate white sauces of Tuscany, to the rich red sauces of the Bolognese school, to the seafoods of Venice and Liguria and to pizza which was born in Naples.

There are two schools of Italian cuisine, northern and southern. Southern Italian cooking, often called Neapolitan, is centered in Naples. Distinguishing characteristics include an overwhelming preference for tomato, rather than cream sauces, the use of tubular pasta such as macaroni, and the use of olive oil rather than butter as a cooking oil. Southern cooking is probably more familiar in North America, because a larger number of immigrants have come from the south. Northern Italian cooking, often

called Bolognese, is centered in Bologna. Distinguishing characteristics include the use of white cream sauces as well as tomato sauces, the use of flat ribbon-like pasta, and the use of butter as well as olive oil.

Visitors are often drawn to Italy by its rich artistic heritage, but they quickly realize that Italy's culinary arts are an integral part of this heritage and of the life of the Italian people. It has been said that Italian art was created to be enjoyed rather than pondered and this goes double for the culinary arts. Wherever one goes in Italy—from the rusty hills of Tuscany with their silvery mantle of olive trees, to the azure coast of Liguria—one is struck by the deep love of life radiated by the people of this splendid land. It is this spirit that shines in each of the following recipes.

THE BASICS

INGREDIENTS

Balsamic Vinegar: A dark brown, sour-sweet wine vinegar that has been aged and decanted over a minimum of five years, often longer.

Basil: A leafy, pungent, frequently-used herb; gives *pesto* sauce its green color.

Butter: A yellow solid spread churned from cow's milk or cream. Used as a cooking oil. When butter is called for in the recipes, it refers to unsalted butter.

Garlic: Undoubtedly the primary seasoning in Italian cuisine, the garlic bulb grows underground producing a head of garlic cloves. Raw garlic has a sharp flavor. Cooked, it loses some of its bite and becomes sweeter and less pervasive. Choose garlic that is firm and tightly closed with skin that is white or white with a purplish cast. It is best stored out of the refrigerator, uncovered in a basket or hanging in a braid.

Mozzarella: A fresh, smooth, unsalted Neapolitan cheese traditionally made from full cream buffalo milk. It is shaped like a ball and used in appetizers, pizza, and pasta dishes.

Olive Oil: Olive oil is extracted from the area just beneath the skin of the olive. The mature olives are picked by hand, then placed in the sun to dry for a short period of time. The olives are then cold pressed between manually-operated grinding wheels. The oil that is extracted during the first pressing is the highest grade olive oil and known as Extra Virgin. There are four types of olive oil, (listed in order of quality): Extra Virgin Olive Oil (of the finest quality), Superfine Virgin Olive Oil, Fine Virgin Olive Oil, and Olive Oil which includes all pressings following the virgin grade. Containing iron and Vitamin A, olive oil is the closest in chemical composition to the fat in human milk and so is the most easily digested and assimilated of all fats and oils.

Oregano: A pungent herb of southern Italian cuisine, oregano is used in many dishes. Neapolitans use it to season their pizza. The flavor is more delicate than thyme and not as sweet as marjoram.

Pancetta: An Italian bacon that is cured with salt and spices but not smoked like American bacon. It should be sliced paper thin for *crostino* or cut up for sauces and stuffings.

Parmigiano-Reggiano (Parmesan): A yellow, hard dry cheese with a rich, sharp flavor made from skimmed cow's milk. Produced only in the strictly controlled area of Emilia-Romagna in the provinces of Parma, Modena, and Reggio Emilia, as well as the province of Mantua. This should be freshly grated at the stove or the table for use as a seasoning. Also a slicing cheese.

Polenta: Semi-course ground corn which resembles semolina (wheat). It is enjoyed throughout Italy cooked as a soft mush or served hard.

Prosciutto: A carefully shaped pork leg, neither cooked nor smoked. It is air-cured for 400 days with sea salt and water, and the salt is periodically washed off so the meat stays sweet and fragrant. Parma ham is Italy's true prosciutto.

Rice: Considered a staple in the north, rice is served boiled plain, with stock, or combined with mushrooms, peas, meat, or fish. Arborio-type Italian rice has short, fat, round grains that are very absorbent yet remain firm when properly cooked. Arborio is the rice of choice by many chefs for *risotto* because it makes a creamy sauce when it's cooked. American short-grain rice may be substituted, but the result will be inauthentic.

Ricotta: A fresh, moist, unsalted cottage cheese used for cooking and in pastries.

Romano: A spicy, sharp and strong cheese. Not a good table cheese, mostly used for grating.

Rosemary: A perennial Mediterranean herb that grows very well in the garden. Its flavor is strong and earthy and works well with grilled or roasted pork, turkey, chicken, veal, or lamb.

Tomatoes: There's nothing like fresh vine-ripened tomatoes. Canned tomatoes like the pear-shaped variety are called Roma in the supermarket. The imported Italian canned tomatoes are called San Marzano and are grown near Naples. Commercial tomato paste is available in convenience cans and tubes, and good for adding a hint of color or tomato flavor.

The Regions of *Italy*

UTENSILS

Cheese Grater: Important for recipes that call for grated hard Italian cheeses like Parmesan and Romano, often used at the table.

Colander: Good for draining pasta and rinsing fresh vegetables.

Garlic Press: A very useful metal device that presses whole garlic cloves into tiny minced pieces.

Knives: A good high carbon steel 10-inch chef's knife and a sharpening steel are a must. Paring knives and a boning knife are also useful.

Peeler: Although some people prefer to leave fruit and vegetable skins on during cooking, peeling is often desirable. When a peeler is used correctly, peeling is effortless and fast.

Pepper Mill: Freshly cracked pepper has much more flavor and aroma than preground pepper. A pepper mill isn't hard to use and the grind may be adjusted to personal taste.

Saucepan with Lid: One saucepan 10 to 12 inches in diameter with a tight-fitting lid will prove indispensable for many of the recipes. Good for sautéing, blanching, preparing sauces, *risotto*, and stews.

Scissors: Excellent for quickly snipping fresh herbs.

Slotted Spoon: Perfect for handling meatballs or small chunky items that must be transferred without broth or sauce.

Spatula: A spatula is good for transferring long flat items such as *scaloppine*. Many chefs prefer wooden spatulas or spoons because they do not scratch teflon or pierce the food.

Stock Pot: A 12-quart stock pot is essential for boiling pasta.

APPETIZERS

Antipasti

Antipasto, literally meaning "before the pasta," is a delicious Italian tradition that promotes conviviality and hints at the greater things to come. A tray of antipasti is set out for guests to serve themselves. Antipasti may be finger foods that are cold, warm, or hot. Some suggestions for antipasti include: thinly sliced meats such as salami, prosciutto, capocollo; hard-cooked eggs; small salted fish such as sardines, chunk tuna, or anchovy fillets wrapped around capers or olives; slices of mozzarella, provolone, Gorgonzola; marinated mushrooms and artichoke hearts; stuffed mushrooms; dry-cured olives; and pickled vegetables.

ANTIPASTO PLATTER

MAKES 8 SERVINGS

6 ounces thinly sliced Genoa salami
6 ounces thinly sliced ham capocollo
6 ounces thinly sliced pepperoni
1 cup Pesto Spread (recipe follows)
1 large tomato
1 8-ounce loaf Italian bread, cut into ¼-inch thick slices
1 pound new potatoes, skins left on, cooked and cut into ¼-inch slices
4 ounces pea pods, trimmed, strings removed
1 red bell pepper, cut into strips
1 small zucchini, cut diagonally into ¼-inch slices
4 ounces fresh mushrooms, sliced
½ cup dry-cured olives (optional)

Prepare Pesto Spread. Cut a ½-inch slice from the top of the tomato. Cut a shallow zigzag edge on the top edge of the tomato. Scoop out the pulp, being careful not to poke a hole in the base of the tomato. Fill the tomato with Pesto Spread; place in the center of a large serving platter. Arrange the Genoa salami, ham capocollo, pepperoni, Italian bread, potatoes, pea pods, red pepper, zucchini, mushrooms, and olives attractively around the tomato.

To serve, spread the slices of bread or potatoes with Pesto Spread and top with sliced meat and assorted vegetables.

Preparation time: 50 minutes
Cooking time: 20 minutes

Antipasto Platter

PESTO SPREAD

MAKES 1 CUP

¾ cup tightly packed fresh
   basil leaves
2 teaspoons freshly chopped
   rosemary, or ¾ teaspoon dried
¼ cup tightly packed Italian parsley
   leaves
2 cloves garlic, quartered
⅓ cup Italian bread crumbs

⅓ cup freshly grated Parmesan
   cheese
1 teaspoon fresh lemon juice
½ teaspoon salt
   Freshly ground black pepper
⅓ cup light cream
⅓ cup olive oil

Combine the basil, rosemary, Italian parsley, and garlic in a food processor bowl fitted with a steel blade; process until blended. Add the bread crumbs, Parmesan cheese, lemon juice, salt, and pepper. With the motor running slowly pour in the cream and olive oil; process until blended. Pour the pesto into a small bowl, cover tightly and refrigerate 1½ to 2 hours to blend the flavors.

Preparation time: 30 minutes
Chilling time: 1½ to 2 hours

ROASTED GARLIC

MAKES 6 SERVINGS

Offer these garlic cloves as part of an antipasto platter. Some people prefer roasting the entire head of garlic with skin intact. Only the very tips of the cloves are sliced off and brushed with olive oil.

12   cloves garlic, peeled
¼   cup olive oil

Preheat oven to 350° F. Place garlic cloves in a small baking dish. Cover the garlic with olive oil and bake for 45 minutes until the garlic is soft.

Preparation time: 5 minutes
Cooking time: 45 minutes

HERB-MARINATED MUSHROOMS

MAKES TWO 8-OUNCE JARS

In Italy, pickled vegetables are a favorite snack food. Perfect for antipasto, these marinated mushrooms are easy to make and delicious.

½   cup white wine vinegar
½   cup olive oil
8   cloves garlic, crushed
½   teaspoon freshly ground black pepper or crushed red pepper
     Salt to taste
8   ounces fresh whole button mushrooms
1   tablespoon chopped fresh herbs of your choice (oregano, thyme, tarragon, basil, dill weed), or
1   teaspoon dried herbs
     Fresh herb sprigs (optional)

In a saucepan combine ¾ cup of water, vinegar, oil, garlic, pepper, and salt. Bring to boil; reduce heat and simmer for 10 minutes. Add mushrooms and chopped herbs; set aside to cool, stirring occasionally. Spoon cooled mushrooms into two 8-ounce jars, packing snugly. Pour the liquid over the mushrooms to cover. Tuck a sprig or two of fresh herb into the jars, if desired. Cover tightly and refrigerate for at least 24 hours. Bring to room temperature before serving.

Preparation time: 15 minutes
Chilling time: 24 hours

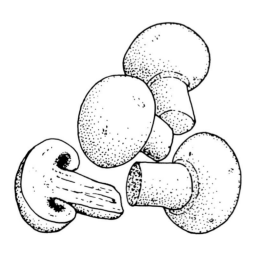

BAGNA CAUDA

MAKES 1 CUP

Although all of Italy delights in this hot, buttery dip flavored with anchovies and garlic, *Bagna Cauda* is credited to the Piedmont district. It is a reliable dip for parties and is a mainstay of Italian New Year's celebrations. The dip should be prepared in a container which can go to the table—flameproof, so that a candle warmer can be set beneath it. It must be kept hot, but never allowed to boil. Serve as a dip for raw or lightly blanched vegetables such as cucumber, fresh mushrooms, celery, zucchini, carrots, cauliflower, green pepper, green onions or bread sticks (*grissini*), another important Piedmontese contribution to Italy's culinary tradition.

Assorted vegetables for dipping
Bread sticks (page 23)
6   *large cloves garlic*
1   *cup sweet butter*
¼   *cup olive oil*
2   *tablespoons chopped anchovies*

Prepare the vegetables and place all but the mushrooms in a bowl of ice water for 1 hour; drain. Wipe mushrooms with a damp cloth. Arrange vegetables on a serving tray and cover with plastic wrap; refrigerate until ready to serve.

Peel garlic; mince or put through a garlic press. Melt the butter in a small saucepan. Add garlic and oil. Cook over very low heat for 5 minutes until garlic is softened but not browned. Add the anchovies and continue cooking for 5 minutes. Serve hot.

Variation: Blend 1 cup of whipping cream and a generous dash or two of freshly ground black pepper into garlic-butter mixture. Simmer for 2 or 3 minutes. Serve hot.

Preparation time: 20 minutes
Chilling time: 1 hour
Cooking time: 12 minutes

PIZZA FRITTATA

MAKES 4 TO 6 SERVINGS

¼   *yellow onion, finely chopped*
¼   *green pepper, finely chopped*
1   *tablespoon butter*
8   *eggs*
2   *ounces thinly sliced pepperoni*
1   *tomato, finely chopped*
½   *teaspoon dried oregano*
¼   *teaspoon salt*
½   *cup shredded mozzarella*

In a 10-inch oven-proof omelet or saucepan, cook the onion and green pepper in butter over medium heat until tender but not browned.

In a bowl, beat together eggs, pepperoni, tomato, oregano, and salt. Pour the egg mixture over the onion and green peppers in the pan. Cook without stirring over low to medium heat until the eggs are set at the edges but still runny in the center, about 7 to 9 minutes.

Sprinkle with cheese. Broil 5 to 6 inches from heat until the cheese melts and browns lightly, about 3 minutes. Cut in wedges to serve.

Preparation time: 10 minutes
Cooking time: 30 minutes

BASIC BRUSCHETTA

MAKES 6 TO 12 SERVINGS

Bruschetta is a small toast grilled over charcoal if possible, and rubbed with garlic then drizzled with extra virgin olive oil. It is also served with a variety of garnishes and toppings. In Abruzzi it may be called *Bruschetta alla Romana*. In Tuscany, a variation known as *crostini* is a regularly served before any meal. Bruschetta may be used as a snack, appetizer, or side dish.

Americans are familiar with something inspired by these little toasts—garlic bread. Garlic bread is Italian bread topped with garlic and melted butter then baked in the oven until crispy.

6 to 12	1-inch thick slices Italian bread
2 to 4	tablespoons olive oil
1 to 2	teaspoons finely chopped garlic

Preheat the oven to 325° F. Arrange the slices of bread on a lightly greased baking sheet and bake on the middle shelf of the oven for about 15 minutes.

Combine the oil and garlic and brush both sides of each slice lightly with the mixture. Then turn the slices over and bake for another 15 minutes, or until lightly browned.

Preparation time: 5 minutes
Cooking time: 30 minutes

Variations: Cut several loaves of bread into 1-inch pieces. Spread 1 to 2 tablespoons of the desired topping on each slice of bread. Bake the bread at 400° F for 6 to 8 minutes, until bread is golden brown and heated through. Serve immediately.

These toppings may also be used to top focaccia and pizzas or rolled into bread doughs before baking. Use what you need and refrigerate the rest for up to a week.

TUSCAN TOPPING

MAKES 3 CUPS

1	cup sun-dried tomatoes in oil, drained and chopped
½	cup toasted pine nuts, coarsely chopped
½	cup minced scallions
1	cup grated Asiago cheese
2	cups shredded provolone cheese

In a bowl, combine the tomatoes, pine nuts, scallions, Asiago, and provolone. Spread 1½ to 2 tablespoons of topping on bread and bake, as directed.

Preparation time: 5 minutes

PESTO TOPPING

MAKES 3 CUPS

1   quart fresh basil leaves,
    washed and dried
2   cups fresh parsley leaves,
    washed and dried
4   cloves garlic
¼   cup toasted pine nuts
1   cup grated Asiago cheese
1   cup olive oil

In a food processor bowl, combine the basil, parsley, garlic and pine nuts. Process until smooth. Add the Asiago and process 30 seconds. Slowly add oil while the motor is running. Spread 2 tablespoons of pesto mixture on bread and bake, as directed.

Preparation time: 5 minutes

Bruschetta with toppings

SOUPS

Zuppe

The course which precedes the meal's main course usually consists of either soup (*zuppa* or *minestra*) or pasta, although in some cases, soup may precede pasta. The term *minestra* is occasionally used to imply a first course of any type. Minestrone, the familiar hearty vegetable soup, is a specific type of *minestra*. Soups are a key part of Italian cuisine, and an important element in meal planning.

BEEF MINESTRONE SOUP

MAKES 6 SERVINGS

Invented in Genoa, this hearty soup is the most well-known of Italian soups, and can stand alone as a main course. In practice, *Minestrone alla Genovese* is usually the most elaborate of Italian minestrones, while *Minestrone alla Milanese* contains rice.

2 tablespoons vegetable oil
6 beef shanks, about
   3 pounds total
1 14½-ounce can beef broth
1 16-ounce can chopped tomatoes
1 stalk celery, sliced into
   ½-inch chunks
1 leek, sliced into
   ½-inch strips
3 cloves garlic, coarsely chopped
2 bay leaves
1 sprig parsley
2 teaspoons dried marjoram

2 teaspoons dried oregano
2 teaspoons dried basil
¼ teaspoon freshly ground black
   pepper
1 pound carrots, sliced into
   ½-inch chunks
1 pound green beans, cut into
   1-inch pieces
   Salt and freshly ground black
   pepper to taste
½ cup freshly chopped parsley
2 ounces Parmesan cheese,
   freshly grated

In a large 8-quart Dutch oven, brown the beef shanks in hot oil, a few at a time. Add the broth, tomatoes, celery, leeks, garlic, bay leaves, parsley, marjoram, oregano, basil, and pepper; mix well. Bring to a boil, stirring occasionally. Reduce heat and cover; simmer soup for 1½ hours, or until the beef is tender. (At this point, the soup may be covered and refrigerated for up to 48 hours.) Add carrots and green beans. Simmer 15 minutes longer, or until the vegetables are tender. Season with salt and pepper.

To serve, place one beef shank in each soup bowl. Ladle soup over shank. Sprinkle with chopped parsley and grated Parmesan cheese.

Preparation time: 25 minutes
Cooking time: 2 hours

At right: Beef Minestrone Soup

PASTA AND CHICKPEA SOUP

MAKES 4 TO 6 SERVINGS

This hearty soup calls for prosciutto from Parma and Parmigiano-Reggiano (Parmesan) cheese from the region in Italy that is authorized by law to make it, Emilia-Romagna. Of course, substitutions are a cook's right, but Italians will tell you that these ingredients are the best in the world.

⅛ pound Parma prosciutto, thinly sliced
1 small red onion, cut into small chunks
1 medium carrot, cut into small chunks
1 stalk celery, cut into small chunks
1 large clove garlic
1½ teaspoons fresh rosemary or ¾ teaspoon dried
¼ cup olive oil
1 28-ounce can Italian plum tomatoes
1 28-ounce can chickpeas, drained
4 cups chicken broth
1 tablespoon tomato paste
1 bay leaf
1 4-inch piece of Parmigiano-Reggiano rind (optional)
   Salt and freshly ground black pepper, to taste
1 cup small pasta tubes (ditali)
1 cup freshly grated Parmigiano-Reggiano cheese (Parmesan)

Finely chop together the Parma prosciutto, red onion, carrot, celery, garlic, and rosemary and combine in a medium-sized bowl.

Set a 3-quart Dutch oven over medium heat and add olive oil. When the oil is hot, add the chopped mixture and cook 10 minutes until the vegetables are softened. Place the tomatoes and their juice into a food processor and chop coarsely. Add to the sautéed vegetables along with the drained chickpeas, chicken broth, tomato paste, bay leaf, and Parmigiano-Reggiano rind. Season with salt and pepper to taste. Stir.

Bring the soup to a gentle simmer and cook for 30 minutes, stirring occasionally. Remove the softened Parmigiano-Reggiano rind, cut it into ¼-inch cubes and return to the soup.

Just before serving, add the pasta to the simmering soup. When the pasta is *al dente*, ladle the soup into bowls and sprinkle generously with freshly grated Parmigiano-Reggiano. Serve immediately.

Preparation time: 10 minutes
Cooking time: 50 to 55 minutes

CREAMY EGGPLANT SOUP

MAKES 4 SERVINGS

Eggplant is one of the best-loved vegetables in Italy. First for the ease with which it grows. Next for its color. And yes, for its versatility.

1   tablespoon vegetable oil
2   medium carrots, thinly sliced
¾   cup yellow onion,
     coarsely chopped
1   clove garlic, minced
1   eggplant (about 1 pound),
     peeled and diced
2   cups chicken broth
¼   teaspoon salt
1   medium potato, cut into
     ¼-inch chunks
1   cup skim evaporated milk
     Freshly ground black pepper
     to taste

Heat oil in 3-quart saucepan. Add the carrot, onion, and garlic. Cook over medium-high heat until vegetables are tender, about 3 to 4 minutes. Add the eggplant, broth, and salt; bring to a boil, stirring occasionally. Reduce heat; cover and simmer about 15 minutes. Add the potato and cook 15 minutes longer, or until potato is tender. Mash vegetables slightly. Stir in the evaporated milk and warm through. Season with freshly ground black pepper.

Preparation time: 7 to 10 minutes
Cooking time: 40 minutes

TORTELLINI SOUP

MAKES 6 SERVINGS

3   tablespoons butter
2   cloves garlic, minced
2   stalks celery, thinly sliced
1   carrot, thinly sliced
4   cups chicken broth
2   cups water
10 ounces cheese-filled tortellini
1   tablespoon freshly chopped
     parsley
     Freshly ground black pepper
     to taste
     Freshly grated Parmesan cheese

Melt butter in a Dutch oven over medium-high heat. Sauté the garlic, celery, onion, and carrot for 10 minutes. Add chicken broth and water and bring soup to a boil. Reduce heat and add tortellini. Cover and simmer, stirring occasionally, until tortellini are *al dente*. Stir in parsley and pepper. Cover and cook for 10 minutes. Serve into soup bowls and sprinkle with Parmesan cheese.

Preparation time: 5 minutes
Cooking time: 40 to 45 minutes

PIZZA, CALZONE, AND BREADS
Pizza, Calzone e Pane

Many of the basic elements of Italian cuisine that are familiar in North America originated in Naples. None of these has become more of a staple across the Atlantic than pizza. Having originated in the sixteenth century, pizza was probably first prepared in the humble homes of the poor. It was an unleavened bread topped with various sauces, cheeses and, if possible, meats. The cheese and tomato variation has always been known in Italy simply as Pizza Margherita.

Eventually the love of pizza spread to other parts of Italy and to Italian communities overseas. In the 1960s, pizza began to become popular as a fast food in North America, and it has become a multi-billion dollar industry with pizzerias representing ten percent of all restaurants.

HOMEMADE PIZZA DOUGH

MAKES 3 12-INCH PIZZAS

1	package (¼ ounce) active dry yeast
¼	cup warm water (110° F)
1	tablespoon sugar
¼	cup olive oil
3½	cups all-purpose flour
1	tablespoon salt

In a small bowl, dissolve yeast and sugar in warm water (110°). Set aside for 5 minutes. In a large mixing bowl, combine the flour and salt. Stir oil into the yeast mixture and stir well.

Gradually stir flour mixture into yeast mixture to form a soft dough. If dough is too dry add a little warm water. Knead dough in mixing bowl until a compact ball is formed. Turn the dough onto a lightly floured surface and knead vigorously until it is smooth and elastic. Put 1 teaspoon olive oil into a bowl. Place dough in bowl and turn twice to coat with oil. Cover with plastic wrap and a kitchen towel and set in a warm place until double in bulk (about 1¼ hours).

After dough has risen, punch dough down and turn out onto work surface. Knead dough for 2 minutes. Divide the dough into three approximately 9-ounce portions. Each portion will make a 12-inch round pizza. Store, tightly wrapped in in the refrigerator for up to 24 hours.

Preheat oven to 475° F. Lightly oil a 12-inch round pan or cookie sheet and dust with cornmeal. Either roll out or press by hand each portion into pan. Assemble the pizza as desired. Bake on the lower rack in a preheated oven for 10 to 12 minutes or until crust is brown and toppings are bubbly.

Preparation time: 5 minutes
Rising and Baking time: 1 hour 45 minutes

Pizza Margherita

FOUR CHEESE PIZZA

MAKES 6 SERVINGS/1 12-INCH PIZZA

1¼ cups crushed tomatoes or sauce tomatoes

3 tablespoons grated Parmesan cheese

¼ teaspoon crushed basil leaves

¼ teaspoon crushed oregano leaves

9 ounces pizza dough (page 20)

¾ cup sliced mushrooms

¼ cup grated Asiago cheese

⅓ cup chopped green peppers

¾ cup shredded provolone cheese

1 cup shredded mozzarella cheese

Preheat oven to 400° F. Prepare the sauce by mixing the crushed tomatoes with Parmesan, basil, and oregano. Shape dough into a 12-inch round crust. Ladle sauce over crust and spread evenly to within ½-inch of the edge. Top the pizza as follows: mushrooms, Asiago, green peppers, provolone, and mozzarella.

Bake 18 to 22 minutes, until crust is crisp and golden. Cut into 6 wedges. Serve hot.

Preparation time: 25 minutes
Cooking time: 18 to 22 minutes

SAUSAGE PIZZA

MAKES 6 SERVINGS/1 14-INCH PIZZA

1	pound mildly seasoned fresh pork sausage
1	cup chopped green pepper
1	cup Marinara Sauce (page 25)
1	6-ounce can tomato paste
1½	teaspoons fennel seed
1	teaspoon sugar
¼	teaspoon dried oregano
12	ounces pizza dough (page 20)
2	cups shredded provolone
2	cups seeded and chopped tomatoes
2	cups shredded mozzarella cheese

Preheat oven to 375° F. In a medium-sized skillet, brown the pork sausage with the green pepper over medium-high heat; drain well. Stir in the tomato sauce, tomato paste, fennel seed, sugar, and oregano. Simmer for 5 minutes.

Using a 14-inch pizza pan or a 15 × 10-inch jelly roll pan, press the dough into shape. Crimp the dough to form a rim.

Layer the provolone, sausage mixture, tomatoes, and mozzarella on the pizza crust. Bake on the lowest rack of the oven for 35 to 45 minutes, or until the crust is golden brown and the cheese is melted.

Preparation time: 20 minutes
Cooking time: 45 minutes

CALZONE

MAKES 6 SERVINGS

The name calzone, meaning "trouser leg," is probably derived from its appearance. In substance, it is a near relative of pizza, and one school of thought holds that it was invented by accident when a pizza got folded upon itself. Like pizza, calzone was born in or near Naples, but the basic Neapolitan style is complemented by other variations such as that from Apulia which includes olives and onions.

6	6-ounce portions pizza dough (page 20)
1	tablespoon olive oil
1	cup coarsely chopped onion
1	clove garlic, crushed
2	cups finely-diced cooked ham
8	ounces ricotta cheese
1	cup grated mozzarella cheese
¼	cup chopped fresh parsley
¼	teaspoon freshly ground black pepper

Heat oil in small skillet and sauté onion and garlic for 5 minutes over medium heat. Spoon onion mixture into a medium-sized bowl with the ham, ricotta, mozzarella, parsley, and pepper. Mix well. Divide onto 6 dough circles. Fold half of each circle over and seal with a fork on the edges. Place on a greased baking sheet. Bake at 400° F for 15 to 18 minutes.

Preparation time: 5 minutes
Cooking time: 20 minutes

PIZZA MARGHERITA

MAKES 4 TO 6 SERVINGS/1 10-INCH PIZZA

1   large tomato (8 ounces)
6   ounces pizza dough (page 20)
4   ounces shredded mozzarella
    cheese
1   tablespoon grated Parmesan
    cheese
⅛   teaspoon salt
    Cornmeal
¼   cup fresh basil leaves,
    thinly sliced
    Salt and freshly ground black
    pepper to taste
    Extra virgin olive oil

Preheat the oven to 450° F. Core the tomato and cut it in half horizontally. Squeeze gently to remove seeds and coarsely chop; set aside.

On a pizza stone or in a pan lightly dusted with cornmeal, press the dough into a 10-inch circle; crimp the edges together to form a rim. Sprinkle with the cheeses and tomato. Season with salt and pepper.

Bake the pizza until crust is crisp and golden, about 10 to 15 minutes. Sprinkle with basil. Drizzle with extra virgin olive oil, if desired.

Preparation
Cooking tim

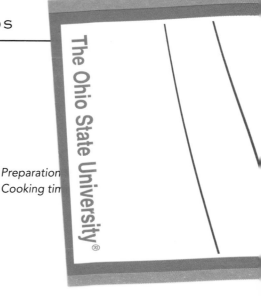

The Ohio State University®

BREAD STICKS

MAKES 4 DOZEN

1   package (¼ ounce) active
    dry yeast
2   cups warm water
2   teaspoons salt
5 to 5½   cups sifted all-purpose flour
1   egg
1   tablespoon milk
    Coarse salt (optional)

Soften yeast in ¼ cup warm water. Set aside. In a large bowl, combine remaining 1¾ cups warm water and salt. Blend in 3 cups flour. Stir softened yeast and add to flour mixture, mixing well. Add about half the remaining flour to the yeast mixture and beat until very smooth. Mix in enough remaining flour to make a soft dough. Turn the dough onto a lightly floured surface. Let rest 5 to 10 minutes. Knead 5 to 8 minutes, until dough is smooth and elastic. Roll dough into a smooth ball and place in a greased bowl, just large enough to allow the dough to double. Turn dough to bring greased surface to the top. Cover bowl with waxed paper and a towel. Let stand in a warm place (about 80° F) until dough is doubled (1½ to 2 hours).

When dough has doubled, punch down with fist. Knead on a lightly

floured surface about 2 minutes. Lightly roll the dough into rectangles about ¼-inch thick and 6 inches wide. Cut dough crosswise with a floured knife into 1-inch wide strips. With the palms of your hands, roll the strips to pencil thickness, stretching them to about 7 inches. Place the strips 1 inch apart on 3 or 4 greased baking sheets.

Slightly beat egg and combine with milk. Brush the dough strips with the egg mixture. Let rise in a warm place until doubled (about 1 hour). Preheat oven to 400° F. Brush again with egg mixture and sprinkle with coarse salt. Bake 18 to 20 minutes or until sticks are browned and crisp.

Preparation time: 3 hours
Cooking time: 18 to 20 minutes

PASTA, RICE, AND POLENTA

Pasta, Riso, e Polenta

Pasta is the keystone of Italian cuisine. In its many forms, pasta is a staple on every Italian table and on the menu at every Italian restaurant in Italy, and around the world. It might be said that no Italian meal is complete without pasta, although that is not necessarily true, and in actual practice, pasta is usually a first or second, rather than main, course.

Made from durum wheat, pasta is an energy-giving complex carbohydrate that is low in fat and high in digestibility. With a higher percentage of protein (13 percent) than potatoes, it contains six of the eight essential amino acids. A four-ounce serving is the caloric equivalent of two small apples.

Pasta was invented independently in both Italy and the Far East. Although it has been incorrectly suggested that Marco Polo introduced pasta to Italy, when he returned to Venice from his epic journey to China at the end of the thirteenth century, in fact, pasta was familiar to the great explorer before he left home.

By the time of the Renaissance, pasta had become an integral part of Italian meal planning, having reached the status that it enjoys to this day.

There are well over 75 individual types of pasta in Italy. These are generally divided into four groups: narrow round noodles (such as spaghetti and vermicelli), flat noodles (such as fettuccine and lasagna), tubular pasta (such as maccheroni and penne), and filled pasta (such as ravioli and tortellini).

Regionally, the cuisine of northern Italy and Sardinia is more likely to include dishes featuring flat noodles, while tubular pasta, especially macaroni (maccheroni), is typically found on the tables of southern Italy and Sicily.

Sauces for pasta are as many and as varied as the pasta itself and here again, regional differences emerge. In the north typical sauces include: *Alfredo* (cream), *alla Bolognese* (meat sauce of the Bologna-style), and *al Burro* (butter). Southern sauces include: *Pesto* (basil, garlic, pine nuts, Parmesan cheese, and olive oil), *Pizzaiola* (tomato and garlic), *Pomodoro* (tomato), *Verde* (green), and *alla Vongole* (clams).

Included in this section, you will find a recipe for making your own pasta from scratch, which is delectable and not very difficult. Fresh pasta cooks in considerably less time than commercial pasta and should be cooked until firm yet tender, or *al dente*, which literally means "to the tooth." Dried and commercially packaged pasta is perfectly acceptable for any of these recipes and will make a fine substitute. There is also a recipe for homemade ravioli.

Each of the other recipes in this section calls for a specific type of pasta, but you may wish to have some fun by substituting similar varieties. Spaghetti and vermicelli may, for example, be interchanged with one another, or with capellini (angel hair), farfelle (bow ties), fettuccine, linguine, penne, ruote (cartwheels), spaghettini, tortellini, or even ravioli.

Riso (rice) is a northern Italy favorite and is served as part of many recipes from the slowly boiled plain *riso* to more elaborate versions combined with mushrooms, meat, fish, or stock. The most famous rice dish is *risotto*, a rice mixture that is served as a main or side dish. Some chefs swear that risotto is impossible to make without using short-grain Italian Arborio rice, but well-respected American chefs have turned out delicious risotto using USA short-grain rice.

From a nutritional standpoint, rice is low in calories and is an excellent source of complex carbohydrates. Rice is economical and easy to prepare. Its mild flavor makes it the ideal companion for subtly flavored foods like seafood and chicken, and for spicy foods like hot sausage.

Polenta is made from semi-course ground corn and resembles semolina which is made from wheat. Like rice, polenta may be served as a main or side dish.

Homemade Pasta

MARINARA SAUCE

MAKES 1 QUART

This tomato sauce is smooth and velvety thanks to a quick pass through a food processor. "Sailor" sauce, as it is called, is the traditional base cooked by Italian fishermen. Light and easy to prepare, it is not usually eaten plain, but flavored with the day's fresh catch.

2	pounds fresh tomatoes, chopped
2	tablespoons olive oil
1	cup chopped yellow onion
2	cloves garlic, minced
1	tablespoon fresh basil, thinly sliced
¼	teaspoon dried oregano
1	teaspoon salt
1	16-ounce can whole Italian peeled tomatoes

Chop the tomatoes; set aside. In a saucepan, heat oil until hot. Add onion and garlic; sauté for about 3 minutes. Add basil, oregano, salt, and chopped tomatoes. Simmer, covered, until the tomatoes are softened, about 10 minutes. Cool slightly.

Place the Italian tomatoes and liquid in a blender or food processor bowl fitted with a steel blade. Cover and process until coarsely chopped. Add tomato sauce; cover and process until almost smooth.

Preparation time: 5 minutes
Cooking time: 15 minutes

HOMEMADE PASTA

MAKES 2½ POUNDS PASTA

3   cups durum or all-purpose flour
¾   cup water (approximately)

TO MAKE BY HAND:
Combine the flour and enough water to make a tight dough. Knead with your hands until dough is smooth and elastic. Form into a ball and lightly oil top. Let rest, covered, 5 to 10 minutes.

Divide the dough into 4 parts. On a floured surface, roll out to ⅓-inch thickness by hand. Let air dry on floured board about 1 hour, turning once.

Dust dough with flour. Roll up like a jelly roll, flatten the top slightly and cut with a sharp knife across the roll into desired widths. After cutting the entire roll, open up the ribbons and spread noodles on a clean towel. Let dry for about 5 minutes before cooking, or wrap in plastic and refrigerate.

USING A MACHINE:
Combine flour and enough water to make a tight dough. Knead or work through pasta machine until smooth and elastic. Let rest, covered, 5 to 10 minutes.

Divide into 4 parts and roll out to ⅓-inch thickness with a pasta ma-

chine. Let air dry on a floured board about 1 hour, turning once. Cut according to desired width and let dry. Pasta may be cooked immediately or wrapped in plastic and refrigerated for later use.

TOMATO PASTA: Add a 16-ounce can of tomato paste to 3 cups of durum flour and enough water to make a tight dough.

SPINACH PASTA: Add ½ cup of spinach to 3 cups of durum flour and enough water to make a tight dough. Canned spinach will do, but fresh or frozen spinach makes a more attractive dough.

HERB PASTA: Use ¼ cup chopped herbs of your choice or ¼ cup chopped fresh parsley and 1 teaspoon fresh dill weed in 3 cups durum flour and approximately ¾ cup of water to make a tight dough.

Preparation time: 2 hours

SPAGHETTI ALLA CARBONARA

MAKES 8 SERVINGS

Coal miners are credited with the invention of this dish. The eggs, pancetta, and cheese make it a hearty first course.

1   pound spaghetti
5   ounces pancetta (bacon), diced
1   tablespoon olive oil
4   eggs
2   tablespoons heavy cream
3½ ounces freshly grated
    Romano cheese
    Salt and freshly ground pepper
    to taste

Boil water in a deep stock pot. Salt water just before adding spaghetti. Stir with a wooden fork to prevent pasta from sticking. Cook for 8 to 10 minutes or until *al dente.*

Meanwhile sauté the bacon in oil. Drain on paper towels. In a bowl, beat the eggs, heavy cream, grated Romano, salt and pepper until

smooth. Drain the spaghetti. Transfer to a warm serving bowl, pour all the egg mixture and pancetta over the pasta and mix thoroughly. Serve immediately.

Preparation time: 5 minutes
Cooking time: 8 to 10 minutes

LINGUINE WITH GARLIC CLAM SAUCE

MAKES 4 TO 6 SERVINGS

This is a quick and easy recipe that allows for many variations. Add some white wine, finely chopped green onions, or, for a spicier flavor, add ¼ teaspoon crushed dried red pepper to the sauce before simmering.

1 pound linguine
¾ cup olive oil or butter
4 or more cloves fresh garlic, minced
3 6½-ounce cans chopped clams, drained, liquid reserved
¼ teaspoon salt
¼ teaspoon freshly ground black pepper
¼ teaspoon fresh thyme
¼ cup chopped parsley

Boil water in a deep stock pot. Salt water just before adding linguine. Stir with a wooden fork to prevent pasta from sticking. Cook for 8 to 10 minutes or until *al dente.*

Meanwhile, heat oil in a large skillet over moderately high heat. Add the garlic and sauté until golden brown, being careful not to burn the garlic. Add the juice drained from clams, salt, pepper, and thyme. Simmer slowly to blend flavors. Add the clams and cook until heated through. While the pasta is cooking, stir parsley into the clam sauce. Just before pasta is done, gently reheat the sauce until it bubbles. Drain the linguine and pour the sauce over it. Serve immediately.

Preparation time: 5 minutes
Cooking time: 8 to 10 minutes

LINGUINE WITH ITALIAN SAUSAGE

MAKES 4 SERVINGS

1 tablespoon oil
½ cup thinly sliced celery
1 yellow onion, finely chopped
1 clove garlic, minced
1 14½-ounce can whole tomatoes, broken up
1 teaspoon dried basil
¼ teaspoon salt
⅛ teaspoon freshly ground black pepper
1 pound fresh Italian sausage, cut into 4 pieces
½ pound linguine

Heat the oil in a 2-quart saucepan over medium-high heat. Add the celery, onion, and garlic and sauté for 3 minutes. Stir in the tomatoes, basil, salt, and pepper. Bring the sauce to a boil, then reduce the heat and cook slowly for 20 minutes, stirring occasionally.

Meanwhile place the sausage and 2 tablespoons of water in a large frying pan. Cover tightly and cook slowly for 10 to 12 minutes, turning once. Uncover and increase the heat to medium. Cook the sausage until cooked through and browned, turning occasionally.

Boil water in a deep stock pot. Salt water just before adding linguine. Stir with a wooden fork to prevent pasta from sticking. Cook for 8 to 10 minutes or until *al dente.* Drain. Place the linguine on a warm platter and top with sausage and tomato sauce.

Preparation time: 10 minutes
Cooking time: 25 minutes

LASAGNA

MAKES 8 SERVINGS

Lasagna is an elegant, satisfying dish. The basic recipe is made with tomato sauce, cream sauce, and three cheeses, all layered between flat, broad noodles. Variations on the theme include chicken, Italian sausage, and spinach. Even spinach noodles could be substituted for the egg noodles making a *Lasagna Verde*.

2 tablespoons cooking oil
1 yellow onion, chopped
1 4-ounce can mushroom pieces
1 28-ounce can Italian-style tomatoes, cut into pieces
1 8-ounce can tomato sauce
1 teaspoon dried oregano
1 teaspoon dried basil
1½ cups ricotta or cottage cheese
½ pound mozzarella cheese, shredded
½ cup freshly grated Parmesan cheese
3 eggs, beaten
2 tablespoons sour cream
1 teaspoon salt
¼ teaspoon freshly ground black pepper
1 8-ounce package lasagna noodles, cooked, or fresh lasagna noodles, uncooked

Heat oil in a skillet over high heat. Sauté the onion and mushrooms about 3 minutes. Add the tomatoes, tomato sauce, oregano, and basil; simmer about 15 minutes.

Preheat oven to 375° F. In a bowl, mix together the cottage cheese, mozzarella, half of the Parmesan cheese, eggs, sour cream, salt, and pepper. Grease a large, shallow baking dish and pour a little of the tomato sauce in the bottom. Add a layer of lasagna noodles; add some of the cheese mixture and then tomato sauce. Repeat layers, ending with sauce. Sprinkle the remaining Parmesan cheese on top and bake for 40 minutes, or until hot and bubbly.

Preparation time: 50 minutes
Cooking time: 1 hour

CHICKEN LASAGNA: Add the meat from 1 chicken (4 cups), cut into bite-sized pieces. To assemble lasagna, cover noodles with pieces of chicken, cheese mixture, and tomato sauce. Continue with recipe.

To cook the chicken, first cut it into parts and place in a Dutch oven with 2 cups of water, 1 small quartered onion, 1 rib of celery with leaves, 1 teaspoon salt, and ¼ teaspoon freshly ground black pepper. Cover and simmer about 45 minutes, or until a fork can be inserted in chicken with ease. Remove chicken from stock and let cool. Remove meat from the chicken and cut into bite-sized pieces; set aside. Discard the bones and skin. Refrigerate stock overnight; skim fat. Reserve for use in other sauces and soups.

ITALIAN SAUSAGE LASAGNA: Add 1 pound bulk Italian sausage, cooked, and well drained. To assemble lasagna, cover noodles with crumbled sausage, cheese mixture, and tomato sauce. Continue with recipe.

SPINACH LASAGNA: Add 1 10-ounce package frozen spinach, cooked, and well drained or 1 bunch fresh spinach, cleaned, cooked and drained. Add spinach and ⅛ teaspoon nutmeg to ⅓ of the cheese mixture. To assemble lasagna, cover noodles with spinach mixture, cheese mixture, and tomato sauce. Continue with recipe.

MOSTACCIOLI WITH MEAT SAUCE

MAKES 6 SERVINGS

2 tablespoons olive oil
1 pound ground beef
¼ cup coarsely chopped green pepper
¼ cup coarsely chopped celery
¼ cup coarsely chopped yellow onion
4 to 5 cloves garlic, minced, depending on personal taste
½ pound thinly sliced mushrooms

1 28-ounce can Italian plum tomatoes
1 6-ounce can tomato paste
½ cup dry red wine
1 teaspoon dried basil
1 teaspoon dried oregano
1 pound mostaccioli, rigatoni, or spaghetti
Freshly grated Parmesan cheese

Heat oil in a large skillet over high heat. Add the beef, pepper, celery, onion, and garlic; cook until the beef is browned. Add the mushrooms; cook until wilted. Add the tomatoes, tomato paste, red wine, basil, and oregano. Stir, crushing the tomatoes with a wooden spoon. Simmer over low heat for 30 minutes, stirring occasionally.

In a large pot, bring salted water to a boil. Cook the mostaccioli for 8 to 10 minutes or until *al dente*. Serve the pasta topped with sauce. Pass the Parmesan cheese.

Preparation time: 10 minutes
Cooking time: 40 minutes

Chicken Lasagna

PASTA PRIMAVERA WITH ROTELLI

MAKES 6 TO 8 SERVINGS

1   pound uncooked rotelle
3   pounds fresh tomatoes
2   tablespoons vegetable oil
½   cup chopped yellow onion
1   cup diced zucchini
1   cup broccoli, cut in small florets
2½ teaspoons oregano
1½ teaspoons salt
⅛   teaspoon freshly ground
    black pepper
1   bay leaf
    Freshly ground Parmesan cheese
    (optional)

In a large pot, bring salted water to a boil. Cook the pasta in boiling water until *al dente*. Drain.

Meanwhile, dice tomatoes; set aside. In a saucepan, heat oil until hot. Add the onion, zucchini, and broccoli; sauté until the vegetables are soft, about 8 to 10 minutes.

Add oregano, salt, black pepper, bay leaf, and tomatoes. Simmer, uncovered, until the sauce is thickened, about 10 to 15 minutes; stir occasionally. Discard the bay leaf from sauce. Toss the pasta with sauce and serve with Parmesan cheese, if desired.

Preparation time: 12 minutes
Cooking time: 18 to 25 minutes

PENNE ARRABBIATA

MAKES 8 SERVINGS

Calabria, in the toe of Italy, has a culinary heritage influenced by the Greeks and the Arabs. It is one of the few regions that favors the use of hot peppers. *Arrabbiata* means "enraged," and lends its name to this spicy sauce.

1   pound uncooked penne
1   pound ripe tomatoes
2   tablespoons olive oil
1   yellow onion, finely diced
7   ounces pancetta (bacon),
        diced
½ to 1 whole hot red pepper,
        depending on personal taste
2   cloves garlic, crushed
¼   cup finely-chopped fresh basil
        Salt to taste
¼   cup freshly grated Pecorino
        Romano cheese

In a large pot, bring salted water to a boil. Cook the penne in boiling water until *al dente*. Meanwhile, in a saucepan boil the tomatoes until they're soft enough to remove the skin. Remove and slice into small pieces leaving the seeds and core intact; set aside.

Heat the oil and sauté the onion, pancetta, hot pepper, and garlic over medium-high heat. When the onion begins to brown, add the tomatoes and basil. Cook uncovered for several minutes over high heat. Add salt to taste. Remove the hot red pepper. Transfer to a serving bowl big enough to hold the penne. Add half the grated cheese.

Drain the penne and immediately pour into the bowl with sauce. Toss to coat penne with sauce. Pass remaining cheese.

Preparation time: 5 minutes
Cooking time: 8 to 10 minutes

RAVIOLI

MAKES 4 TO 6 SERVINGS

1¼ cups durum or all-purpose flour
1 egg, slightly beaten
  Pinch of salt
½ cup water (approximately)

FILLING

1 pound lean ground beef
½ cup chopped onion
¼ cup chopped celery
⅛ teaspoon garlic, minced
  Salt and freshly ground black
  pepper to taste
1 6-ounce can tomato paste
3 tablespoons grated Romano or
  Parmesan cheese

Combine all of the ingredients by hand or with a mixer to make very firm dough. Refrigerate, covered, 1 hour while making the filling.

In a skillet over high heat, brown the beef and drain. Add the onion, celery, garlic, salt, pepper, tomato paste, and cheese and simmer until vegetables are tender; stir occasionally.

Roll the dough into a ¼-inch thick sheet and cut into 6-inch wide strips. Place a teaspoon of the filling 1 inch from the narrow end and continue putting 1 teaspoon filling at 2-inch intervals across the dough and in columns With a pastry brush dipped in water, brush straight lines between the mounds of filling. Place a second sheet of pastry over the first and

press down between the mounds to seal ravioli tightly. With a ravioli cutter or knife, cut the ravioli into squares. Let stand 30 minutes.

Ravioli can be frozen at this point. Arrange in single layer on a floured cookie sheet. Dust top of the ravioli with flour; cover and freeze until firm, then package in an airtight container.

To cook, drop the ravioli into rapidly boiling salted water and cook, stirring occasionally, until they float. Drain.

Combine any leftover filling with your sauce of choice. Serve ravioli with sauce and grated cheese.

Preparation time: 2 hours
Cooking time: 20 minutes

HAZELNUT MANICOTTI

MAKES 4 TO 8 SERVINGS

8 manicotti shells
1 cup roasted and coarsely
  chopped hazelnuts
1 10-ounce package frozen
  chopped spinach, thawed,
  drained, and pressed
½ cup ricotta or cottage cheese
½ cup green onions, thinly sliced
1 teaspoon garlic, minced
¼ teaspoon nutmeg
¼ teaspoon freshly ground
  pepper
2 eggs, slightly beaten
2 to 3 cups Marinara Sauce (page 25)
  Salt to taste

Preheat oven to 375° F. Cook the manicotti in boiling water until partially softened, about 5 minutes; drain. In a bowl, mix the hazelnuts, spinach, ricotta, onions, garlic, nutmeg, pepper, and eggs. Fill the manicotti with the spinach mixture. Preheat oven to 375° F.

Cover the bottom of a 2-quart baking dish with one cup of the Marinara Sauce. Arrange the filled manicotti in a single layer in the baking dish, allowing space between each for expansion during cooking. Cover with the remaining sauce. Bake for 40 to 45 minutes.

Preparation time: 15 minutes
Cooking time: 45 minutes

RISOTTO WITH PEAS AND MUSHROOMS

MAKES 6 SERVINGS

2   tablespoons margarine
½   cup chopped yellow onion
1   cup Arborio or short-grain rice
⅓   cup dry white wine
1   cup chicken broth
1   cup frozen peas, thawed
1   2½-ounce jar sliced mushrooms, drained
¼   cup grated Parmesan cheese
¼   teaspoon ground white pepper
⅓   cup 2 percent low-fat milk

Bring broth to a boil in a small saucepan and continue to simmer over low heat.

In a large skillet over medium-high heat, cook the onion in margarine until soft. Add rice; stir 2 to 3 minutes coating the grains in margarine. Add wine and stir until absorbed. Stir in broth. Cook, uncovered, stirring constantly, until broth is absorbed. Continue stirring and adding 4 cups of water, one cup at a time; each cup to be absorbed before adding another. Continue until rice is tender and mixture has a creamy consistency, about 20 to 25 minutes.

Stir in peas, mushrooms, cheese, pepper, and milk. Stir until mixture is creamy, about 1 to 2 minutes. Serve immediately.

Preparation time: 5 minutes
Cooking time: 50 minutes

Above: The Palazzo in Sienna
Right: Risotto with Peas and Mushrooms

RISOTTO ALLA MILANESE

MAKES 6 SERVINGS

2 cups beef broth
1 yellow onion, finely chopped
2 tablespoons butter
2 cups Arborio or short-grain rice
⅛ teaspoon crushed saffron
½ cup dry white wine
1 teaspoon salt
⅓ cup freshly grated Parmesan cheese
2 tablespoons finely chopped parsley

Bring broth and 4½ cups of water to a boil in a 3-quart saucepan and continue to simmer over low heat.

Meanwhile in a Dutch oven melt the butter over medium-high heat. Add the onions, stirring continuously and cooking until tender but not browned, about 2 minutes. Add the rice and continue cooking, stirring constantly, for 2 to 3 minutes, or until the rice grains glisten with butter and appear slightly opaque.

In a small bowl, mix ½ cup of the simmering beef broth with the saffron. Add the wine, salt, and saffron mixture to the rice and boil until almost all of the liquid is absorbed. Add the remaining beef broth and water, ½ cup at a time, cooking and stirring after each addition, until the liquid is almost all absorbed and the rice is tender but still firm, about 55 minutes. The risotto should be creamy, not dry or runny.

Remove the risotto from heat. Stir in the cheese and parsley. Serve immediately.

Preparation time: 10 minutes
Cooking time: 1 hour

BAKED POLENTA WITH ASIAGO AND MUSHROOM SAUCE

MAKES 6 SERVINGS

1 teaspoon salt
1½ cups polenta (coarsely ground corn meal)
8 ounces Asiago cheese, grated (about 2 cups)

Preheat the oven to 350° F. In a large saucepan bring 6 cups of water to a boil. Add salt, then add the polenta slowly, stirring constantly. Cook, continuing to stir, until polenta begins to thicken, about 5 minutes. Stir in half the cheese.

Pour the polenta into a buttered 8×8-inch baking pan. Bake uncovered until firm, about 35 minutes. Sprinkle the top with remaining cheese after 25 minutes and return polenta to oven. While the polenta bakes, make the sauce.

Preparation time: 10 minutes
Cooking time: 40 minutes

MUSHROOM SAUCE

MAKES 3 CUPS

1 8-ounce jar roasted bell peppers, drained
1 pound button mushrooms, sliced
2 tablespoons olive oil
2 cups Marinara Sauce (page 25)
1 teaspoon dried rosemary, crushed
¼ cup chopped parsley

Purée the peppers in a food processor or blender and reserve. Over high heat, brown the mushrooms in oil. Transfer to a warm plate and reserve. Add the reserved pepper purée, tomato sauce, rosemary, and 1 cup of water to the pan used for the mushrooms. Simmer over medium heat until the sauce thickens, about 10 minutes. Stir in the reserved mushrooms and parsley.

To serve, cut the polenta into pieces and top with a generous helping of sauce.

Preparation time: 5 minutes
Cooking time: 15 minutes

SEAFOOD
Frutti di Mare

With the longest coastline and largest merchant marine of any country in Europe, there is little wonder that seafood should form such an important part of Italy's culinary culture. From the Ligurian Sea in the west to the Adriatic in the east and the Gulf of Taranto in the south, the fruits of the Italian seas are many and varied.

The catch includes tuna, sole, sea bass, and anchovies as well as such shellfish as clams, mussels, oysters, shrimp, and scampi, whose shrimp-like delicacy is known in its true form only in the central Mediterranean. One joy of the Italian cuisine that is not often shared with the rest of the world is *calamari* (squid), so we've included several recipes on these pages.

SEAFOOD STEW

MAKES 4 TO 6 SERVINGS

From Genoa to Livorno (Leghorn), the fishing towns of the Ligurian coast are noted for their fabulous seafood stews. An entire cuisine has evolved here around seafood and the vegetables raised on the steep hillsides that isolate these towns from the rest of the land.

1   yellow onion, finely chopped
2   cloves garlic, minced
2   tablespoons olive oil
1   cup dry white wine
2   plum tomatoes, diced
¼   cup elbow macaroni
½   teaspoon dried basil
¼   teaspoon crushed hot pepper flakes
1   bay leaf
¼   pound mixed firm fish, such as halibut, sea bass, red snapper, or rockfish, cut into 1½-inch chunks
½   pound raw medium-sized shrimp, peeled and deveined, or 24 scrubbed and debearded mussels, or a combination of both

In a large soup kettle, combine the onion, garlic, and oil; sauté for 5 minutes, or until the onion is soft. Add 2 cups of water, wine, tomatoes, pasta, basil, red pepper, bay leaf, salt, and pepper. Bring to a boil; reduce heat and simmer, partially covered, for 10 minutes.

Add seafood and simmer, covered, 8 to 10 minutes, or until the fish flakes easily when tested with a fork. Before serving, remove and discard bay leaf.

Preparation time: 10 minutes
Cooking time: 35 to 37 minutes

At right: An open-air restaurant in Arezzo

DEEP-FRIED CALAMARI

MAKES 6 SERVINGS

If there is a signature seafood in Italy, it is probably calamari or squid, and it is often enjoyed deep-fried as a snack on warm summer evenings as cool breezes waft in from the sea.

3   pounds calamari, cleaned and cut
     into rings
3   cups flour
     Salt and freshly ground black
     pepper, to taste
3   cups peanut oil
     Lemon-Garlic Butter
     (recipe follows)

Dry the rings thoroughly with paper towels. In a shallow dish, mix flour, salt, and pepper. Dredge the rings in the flour mixture to coat. Heat peanut oil to 350° F in a deep-fat fryer or heavy casserole. If you don't have a temperature control or thermometer, you can guess at the temperature by dropping a few drops of water into the oil. It should sizzle immediately on contact.

Plunge a metal basket laden with one layer of squid into oil. It should bubble vigorously on contact. If you don't have a basket for deep-frying, use a large spoon or tongs to immerse the squid in oil. Fry the squid until its coating turns golden brown, about 3 to 4 minutes.

Remove the squid and drain on paper towels. Turn down the heat to moderate until just before you are ready to cook the next batch, as oil will overheat when the fryer is empty. Serve rings hot with Lemon-Garlic Butter.

Preparation time: 15 minutes
Cooking time: 15 minutes

LEMON-GARLIC BUTTER

MAKES ¼ CUP

     4   tablespoons butter
1 to 6   cloves garlic, minced
       Juice of 2 lemons

Fry the garlic in 1 tablespoon of butter until lightly browned. Add the remaining butter and lemon. When the butter melts, sauce is ready to serve.

Preparation time: 5 minutes

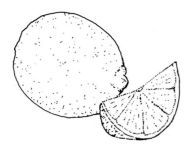

CALAMARI FESTIVAL STYLE

MAKES 6 SERVINGS

3 pounds calamari, cleaned and cut
   into bite-sized pieces
⅓ cup olive oil
¼ cup white wine
¼ cup dry sherry
1 tablespoon crushed fresh garlic
½ lemon
1 teaspoon dried basil, or
   1 tablespoon fresh
1 teaspoon dry oregano, or
   1 tablespoon fresh
¼ teaspoon crushed dry
   red pepper
   Red Sauce (recipe follows)

In a large skillet, heat olive oil on high heat. Add the wine and sherry and sauté crushed garlic. Squeeze the juice of ½ lemon into the pan and place the lemon rind in pan. Sprinkle herbs over mixture and add the calamari. Sauté the calamari for approximately 4 minutes on high heat, stirring occasionally. Do not overcook.

Preparation time: 15 minutes
Cooking time: 6 minutes

RED SAUCE

MAKES 2 CUPS

1 pound whole, peeled tomatoes,
   canned or fresh
1 tablespoon olive oil
½ green pepper, finely chopped
1 stalk celery, finely chopped
1 yellow onion, finely chopped
3 cloves garlic, minced

Mash the tomatoes with a potato masher and set aside. In a medium-sized pan, heat oil. Add the chopped ingredients; sauté until the onion is transparent. Add the mashed tomatoes; simmer for ½ hour. Pour the sauce over the calamari; heat for 1 minute.

Preparation time: 10 minutes
Cooking time: 35 mintues

HOW TO CLEAN CALAMARI

1. Calamari has two parts: the body, called the mantle, and the arms, called tentacles.

2. To clean, hold the mantle in one hand and the head and tentacles in the other. Gently pull your two hands apart.

3. The shell of the calamari is inside the mantle. To remove, grasp the hard "pen or quill," as it is called, between your thumb and forefinger and pull it out.

4. Remove the tentacles from the head by cutting just in front of the eyes.

5. Cut or pop out the round, hard "beak" from the center of the tentacles and discard. The tentacles can be cooked as is, or chopped.

6. Clean the mantle by gently pulling off the fins and peeling off the speckled skin. Turn the mantle inside out and scrape away any remaining viscera with the back of a knife. Wash thoroughly under running water. Prepare the body for cooking by cutting into rings, leaving whole for stuffing or cutting down one side and opening flat for steaks and fillets.

MEATS AND POULTRY
Carne y Pollame

A wide variety of meats has always been available to the Italian palate. The Romans preferred veal to beef, enjoyed mutton, and they enjoyed pork more. One favorite dish, a whole pig stuffed with oysters, was known as Trojan Pork because it was reminiscent of the Trojan Horse of legend. In the economically trying times following the collapse of the Roman Empire, meat became almost a delicacy, and in Florence as late as the fourteenth century, it was served only on Sunday.

By the late fifteenth century, as the city states became more prosperous from their foreign trade, meat once

Picturesque red-tiled Italian residences

again began to form an important part of the Italian diet. Sausage and grilled meats were popular, and veal steaks were being enjoyed with pasta.

Today as in Roman times, the most popular meat is veal, which is known as *vitello* in the north and *vitella* in the south. Latium invented veal *saltimbocca* which means "jump in the mouth" and features a breaded cutlet flavored with sage and topped with ham and mozzarella. Wild game is also popular in many places, partridge and wild boar in particular. Emilia-Romagna is perhaps the greatest gastronomic region in Italy and both Parma and Bologna are within its area. Important cured meats in the Italian diet include ham (*prosciutto*), of which the best comes from Parma. Bologna is an important center for the production of sausages, including mortadella and salami. But other regions have their specialties. Calabria in the toe of Italy makes an excellent *capocolla* that most closely resembles Canadian bacon, and *soprassoto*, a thick spicy sausage with pistachios. The Marches enjoy a dish called *porchetta*, roast pork stuffed with liver and seasoned with fennel, garlic, and sage. Abruzzi and Molise raise sheep for their meat and wool, and ground lamb with green peppers and tomatoes over egg noodles is a favorite dish.

Poultry has always been immensely popular in Italy. Since ancient Roman times, cities and villages alike have always had their poultry markets. Chicken has always been the most important fowl, but the Romans enjoyed wild duck and imported guinea hens—known then as Carthaginian chickens—from Africa. There is even a story about Roman troops driving huge herds of flightless geese home from northern France.

Today, an Italian poultry market is likely to include chickens, ducks, and geese as well as turkey, which was first imported from North America two hundred years ago. Tuscany, for example, is noted for its fine chickens. Wild birds are also popular in Italy, including partridge, quail, pheasant, woodcock, and the wild ducks that the Romans favored. Small birds, such as larks, thrushes, and warblers, are also served, usually grilled on skewers.

Poached Beef Rib Eye Roast

POACHED BEEF RIB EYE ROAST

MAKES 6 SERVINGS

2 pound beef rib eye roast
2 tablespoons vegetable oil
1 10½-ounce can condensed beef broth
1 cup Burgundy wine
2 cloves garlic, minced
1 teaspoon dried marjoram leaves
4 black peppercorns
3 whole cloves
   Herb, Blue Cheese or Mushroom Sauce, if desired (recipes follow)

Tie the beef roast with heavy string at 2-inch intervals. In a Dutch oven brown the roast in oil over medium-high heat until all sides are browned. Pour off the drippings; add 4 cups water, beef broth, wine, garlic, marjoram, peppercorns, and cloves. Bring to a boil; reduce heat to medium-low, cover and simmer for 15 minutes per pound. Temperature should register 130° F. Do not overcook.

Remove the roast to a serving platter, cover tightly with aluminum foil, and allow to stand for 10 minutes before carving. During standing, the roast will rise approximately 10 degrees in temperature to 140° F for rare. Remove the string and carve the roast into thin slices. Serve with desired sauce.

Preparation time: 10 minutes
Cooking time: 20 to 30 minutes

STEAK AND SPAGHETTI SQUASH

MAKES 4 SERVINGS

1¼ pounds beef eye round roast
1 clove garlic, split
½ fresh lemon, cut in half
   lengthwise
2 pounds spaghetti squash
1 pound fresh tomatoes, peeled,
   chopped, and drained
¼ cup finely chopped yellow onion
3 tablespoons freshly chopped
   basil
1 tablespoon freshly chopped
   parsley
¾ teaspoon salt
⅛ teaspoon freshly ground
   black pepper

Cut the roast against the grain into ¼-inch thick steaks. Rub garlic and the juice of 1 lemon quarter evenly on both sides of each steak slice. Place the steaks in a dish; cover and refrigerate until ready to cook.

In a saucepan combine the tomatoes, onion, basil, parsley, ¼ teaspoon salt, pepper, and the juice of the remaining lemon quarter; mix well. Cook until just heated through.

Meanwhile place the squash in boiling water, cover and cook 30 minutes, or until a fork inserted into the flesh slides in easily. Remove the squash and let cool until easy to handle. Cut the squash in half lengthwise and remove the seeds and stringy fibers. Remove the squash flesh by using a fork to pull the flesh out in long strands. Combine the squash strands with ⅔ cup of tomato sauce; set aside and keep warm.

Remove the steaks from the dish. Quickly panbroil the steaks in a large nonstick skillet for 10 minutes. Season with the remaining salt and pepper, or to taste. When steaks are almost done, quickly reheat the tomato mixture.

To serve, place the squash mixture on a large serving platter and arrange the steak slices on top. Spoon the remaining tomato sauce over the steaks.

Preparation time: 15 minutes
Cooking time: 22 minutes

MEATBALLS IN A BASKET

MAKES 8 SERVINGS

2 pounds lean ground beef
2 tablespoons butter or olive oil
1 medium green pepper, chopped
1 medium yellow onion, chopped
1 16-ounce can stewed tomatoes
½ teaspoon dried basil leaves
¼ teaspoon dried thyme leaves
2 tablespoons flour
   Bread Basket (recipe follows)

Shape the ground beef into 1½-inch balls. In a large skillet, lightly brown the meatballs in butter for 5 minutes. Add the green pepper and onion and cook for 5 minutes, stirring occasionally.

Drain the tomatoes, reserving liquid. Add the tomatoes, all but ¼ cup of the tomato liquid, basil and thyme to the meatballs. Cover tightly and cook slowly for 5 minutes.

Combine the reserved tomato liquid with flour, stirring until smooth.

Stir the flour mixture into the meatballs, cover tightly and cook for 5 minutes, or until the sauce thickens.

Meanwhile, prepare the Bread Basket and place it on a warm platter. Spoon the meatball mixture into and around the warm bread.

Preparation time: 10 minutes
Cooking time: 20 minutes

BREAD BASKET

1 16-ounce loaf unsliced
   fresh bread
¼ cup melted butter
¼ cup freshly grated Parmesan
   cheese

Preheat the oven to 400° F. Cut a ¾-inch slice from the top of the bread. With a fork, scoop out the inside of the loaf to form a basket, leaving 1 inch of bread on the sides and bottom. Place the loaf on foil in a shallow baking dish. Brush the top, sides and inside of the bread basket with melted butter. Sprinkle the loaf with Parmesan cheese, coating the sides evenly. Bake for 10 minutes.

Preparation time: 10 minutes
Cooking time: 10 minutes

VEAL MARSALA

MAKES 4 SERVINGS

1 pound veal scallops
¼ cup flour
1 teaspoon salt
¼ teaspoon freshly ground
  black pepper
2 tablespoons olive oil
2 tablespoons butter
1 clove garlic, minced
1 tablespoon tomato paste
½ cup dry Marsala wine
¼ cup red wine
8 ounces fresh mushroom caps
1 teaspoon chopped parsley

Cover the veal with two pieces of wax paper. Using a meat mallet, pound lightly until the veal is ¼-inch thick. In a shallow bowl, combine the flour, salt, and black pepper; dredge the veal in the flour mixture.

Heat the olive oil and butter in a large skillet over medium-high heat. Add the pieces of veal to the skillet until they just cover the bottom without crowding. Cook for 2 to 3 minutes on each side, until the veal pieces are lightly browned. Transfer the veal to a serving platter; keep warm.

Add the garlic to the pan and sauté briefly. In a small bowl, mix the tomato paste with the Marsala and red wine. Add tomato mixture to the skillet. Add mushrooms. Stir to blend with pan juices. Simmer 3 to 5 minutes.

Return the veal to the skillet and heat through. Sprinkle with parsley and serve immediately.

Preparation time: 15 minutes
Cooking time: 10 to 15 minutes

OSSO BUCO

MAKES 6 SERVINGS

Osso Buco is one of the signature dishes of Italy. Made with veal shanks and smothered in a rich sauce of tomato, white wine, finely chopped vegetables, and garnished with lemon zest, it is traditionally served over a bed of creamy *Risotto alla Milanese*. The marrow, considered a great delicacy, is scooped out of the shank bones with a special spoon.

3½ pounds veal shank cross cuts,
  cut 2 inches thick
2 tablespoon olive oil
1 teaspoon salt
½ cup white wine
1 16-ounce can Italian plum
  tomatoes
1 6-ounce can tomato paste
2 teaspoons dried basil
2 teaspoons dried rosemary
¼ teaspoon ground red pepper
¼ teaspoon freshly ground
  black pepper
2 tablespoons butter
1 yellow onion, finely chopped
1 carrot, finely chopped
1 rib celery, finely chopped
2 cloves garlic, minced
3 cups Risotto alla Milanese
  (page 33)
¼ cup finely chopped parsley
1 teaspoon grated lemon peel

Brown half of the veal shanks at a time in oil in a large, heavy skillet over medium heat. Remove the shanks and sprinkle them with salt; set aside.

Pour off the drippings. Add the white wine over high heat. Stir in the tomatoes, tomato paste, basil, rosemary, and red and black pepper. Reduce heat and simmer for 10 minutes.

Meanwhile, in a Dutch oven sauté the onion, carrot, celery, and garlic in butter over medium heat until the vegetables are crisp but tender. Add the shanks and tomato sauce to the Dutch oven. Reduce heat to a simmer and continue cooking, covered, for 2 hours or until the meat is tender.

Meanwhile prepare *Risotto alla Milanese*. Combine the parsley, garlic, and lemon peel. Sprinkle over the veal shanks and sauce. Remove from heat and let stand, covered, for 2 minutes. Serve the *Osso Buco* over *Risotto alla Milanese*.

Preparation time: 30 minutes
Cooking time: 2½ hours

VEAL PICCATA

MAKES 2 SERVINGS

8 ounces veal cutlets, cut ¼ to ⅛-inch thick
4 teaspoons flour
¼ teaspoon salt
⅛ teaspoon freshly ground black pepper
1 tablespoon olive oil
1 clove garlic, minced
¼ cup dry white wine
1 tablespoon fresh lemon juice
2 teaspoons chopped parsley

Place the veal between two pieces of wax paper and flatten with a mallet or the bottom of a small, heavy skillet to ⅛-inch thick or thinner. In a shallow dish, combine the flour, salt, and pepper. Dredge the cutlets in the flour mixture. Heat the oil in a skillet large enough to hold the cutlets in a single layer. Sauté the cutlets over high heat for 1 to 1½ minutes, turning once. Transfer the cutlets to a platter and keep warm.

Add the garlic to the pan drippings and sauté for 30 seconds, stirring constantly. Add the wine and lemon juice; bring to a boil and cook until the sauce is slightly reduced.

Serve the cutlets with the sauce. Sprinkle with parsley.

Preparation time: 10 minutes
Cooking time: 2 minutes

Above: A quaint side street in Genoa
Right: Veal Piccata

VEAL TONNATO

MAKES 6 SERVINGS

This elegant dish of chilled veal with tuna sauce and garnished with capers and lemon slices is often an appetizer but may be a main course as it is here. Pork tenderloins may be substituted for veal.

2 whole veal tenderloins
   (about 1½ pounds total)
½ yellow onion, sliced
1 tablespoon lemon juice
½ teaspoon hot pepper sauce
1 teaspoon pickling spice*
½ teaspoon salt
   Tonnato Sauce (recipe follows)
2 tablespoons drained capers
4 tablespoons chopped parsley
   Lemon slices (optional)

*NOTE: This prepackaged blend of seasonings is available in most markets and varies from manufacturer to manufacturer.

Place the tenderloins, onion, 1½ cups of water, lemon juice, hot pepper sauce, pickling spice, and salt in a large skillet. Bring to a boil; cover and simmer for 20 minutes. Transfer the tenderloins to a platter; cover and refrigerate until 1 hour before serving time. Reserve cooking liquid for Tonnato Sauce and to use in other soups and sauces.

To serve, slice the meat ¼-inch thick. Arrange the slices, slightly overlapping, on a serving platter. Pour the Tonnato Sauce over the veal and garnish with capers, parsley, and lemon slices.

Preparation time: 10 minutes
Cooking time: 20 minutes
Chilling time: 2 hours to overnight

TONNATO SAUCE

MAKES 1½ CUPS

1 6½-ounce can white tuna,
   drained
1 cup mayonnaise
1 tablespoon Dijon-style mustard
2 tablespoons lemon juice

In a blender or food processor combine the tuna, mayonnaise, mustard, and lemon juice; process until smooth. Stir in some of the reserved cooking liquid until the sauce is the consistency of a thick syrup. Cover and refrigerate until serving time.

Preparation time: 5 minutes

LAMB KEBOBS

MAKES 6 SERVINGS

1½ pounds lamb (any cut)
¼   cup Dijon-style mustard
3   tablespoons white wine vinegar
2   tablespoons vegetable oil
⅓   cup shallots, minced
1   teaspoon salt
1   teaspoon thyme
2   large green peppers cut into
    2-inch cubes
4   small boiled onions
½   cup small mushroom caps

Cut the lamb into 2-inch cubes. In a non-aluminum container, combine the mustard, wine vinegar, oil, shallots, salt, and thyme. Reserve ¼ cup marinade. Add the lamb, cover and marinate in the refrigerator for 2 to 24 hours.

Drain the lamb, discarding the marinade. Sauté the mushroom caps over medium heat in reserved ¼ cup of marinade until slightly tender but still firm, about 1 minute. Thread the lamb and vegetables, alternately, onto skewers. Brush the kebobs with marinade. Broil the kebobs for 10 minutes, turning once.

Preparation time: 15 minutes
Marinating time: 2 to 24 hours
Cooking time: 10 minutes

LOIN LAMB CHOPS ROMANA

MAKES 2 SERVINGS

4   4-ounce lean lamb loin chops, well trimmed and cut 1-inch thick
    Salt and freshly ground black pepper to taste
¼   cup olive oil
1   cup sliced green pepper
1   cup diced eggplant
1   cup sliced mushrooms
3   cloves garlic, minced
¼   cup minced yellow onion
½   cup dry white wine
1   tomato, seeded and diced
¼   cup fresh basil

Season the lamb chops with salt and pepper. In a large skillet, heat 2 tablespoons olive oil and sauté the lamb chops over high heat for 3 to 4 minutes on each side, or until browned. Transfer to a warm platter. Add the remaining 2 tablespoons of olive oil to the skillet and sauté the green pepper, eggplant, mushrooms, garlic, and onion for 4 to 5 minutes, or until the onions become transparent.

Stir in the wine. Return lamb chops to skillet and coat with wine sauce. Cover and simmer for 5 to 8 minutes, or until the lamb is cooked to the desired degree of doneness. Lightly sauté the tomato and basil and serve immediately.

Preparation time: 12 minutes
Cooking time: 15 to 21 minutes

ROAST LEG OF LAMB

MAKES 6 SERVINGS

5 to 7   pound leg of lamb
3   cloves garlic, minced
2   teaspoons dried rosemary, crushed
1   teaspoon dried thyme leaves
1   teaspoon dried sage, crushed
½   teaspoon freshly ground black pepper

Preheat oven to 325° F. In a small bowl, combine the garlic, rosemary, thyme, sage, and pepper. Rub the herbs over the surface of the lamb leg. Place the lamb, fat side up, on a rack in an open roasting pan. Insert a meat thermometer so the bulb is centered in the thickest part but not resting in fat or bone. Do not add water. Do not cover. Roast the lamb in a slow oven to desired degree of doneness. Allow 20 to 25 minutes per pound for rare, 25 to 30 minutes for medium, and 30 to 35 minutes for well done.

Remove the roast from the oven when the meat thermometer registers 135° F for rare, 155° F for medium, and 165° F for well done. Allow the roast to stand for 15 to 20 minutes in a warm place before carving.

Preparation time: 10 minutes
Cooking time: 2 hours 20 minutes to 4 hours 5 minutes

STUFFED PORK LOIN GENOVESE

MAKES 10 SERVINGS

½	cup freshly chopped basil
1¼	cups freshly chopped parsley
½	cup pine nuts
6	cloves garlic, finely chopped
½	cup freshly grated Parmesan cheese
½	pound ground pork
½	pound ground Italian sausage
1	cup dry bread crumbs
¼	cup milk
1	egg
1	teaspoon freshly ground black pepper
4 to 5	pound boneless pork loin roast

Preheat oven to 350° F. In a blender or food processor, thoroughly blend the fresh basil, 1 cup of the parsley, pine nuts, garlic, and Parmesan cheese; set aside.

In a bowl, knead together the ground pork, Italian sausage, bread crumbs, milk, egg, the remaining ¼ cup of parsley, and pepper.

Place the roast fat side down on work surface. Spread with the herb and cheese mixture. Place the ground pork mixture along the center of the loin. Fold the roast in half and tie securely with a string. Roast for 1½ hours. Let stand 10 minutes before slicing.

Preparation time: 15 minutes
Cooking time: 1½ hours

PORK WITH ARTICHOKES AND CAPERS

MAKES 4 SERVINGS

1	pound pork tenderloin
2	teaspoons butter
1	small shallot, finely chopped
1	tablespoon capers, drained
¼	cup chicken broth
1	teaspoon Dijon-style mustard
1	cup artichoke hearts, drained, rinsed and halved
4	fresh lemon slices
2	tablespoons chopped parsley

Cut the pork tenderloin crosswise in 8 equal pieces. Press each piece to 1-inch thickness. Heat butter in a non-stick skillet over medium-high heat. Add the pork pieces and cook 3 to 4 minutes on each side, or until the pork is tender. Remove the pork from the skillet and transfer to a serving platter; keep warm.

Reduce heat to low. Add the shallot and capers; cook for 1 to 2 minutes, stirring frequently. Stir in the chicken broth, mustard, and artichokes; cook and stir until thoroughly heated. Spoon the artichoke mixture over the cooked pork pieces. Garnish with lemon slices and sprinkle with freshly chopped parsley.

Preparation time: 20 minutes
Cooking time: 6 to 10 minutes

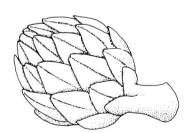

LEAN HOMEMADE SAUSAGE

MAKES 8 SERVINGS

- 1 pound lean ground pork
- ½ teaspoon dried rosemary
- ⅛ teaspoon dried thyme
- ⅛ teaspoon crushed dried marjoram
- ⅛ teaspoon freshly ground black pepper
- ⅛ teaspoon salt
- 1 tablespoon olive oil (optional)

In a large bowl, combine all the ingredients except the oil; mix well. Place in an airtight container and refrigerate for 4 to 24 hours to allow the flavors to blend.

Shape the sausage into ½-inch thick patties. In a skillet, heat the oil and cook the patties over medium heat about 4 to 5 minutes on each side, or until done.

Patties may also be broiled. To broil, place the patties on an unheated rack in a broiler pan. Broil 5 inches from the heat for 5 minutes on each side.

Preparation time: 10 minutes
Chilling time: 4 hours to overnight
Cooking time: 10 minutes

PORK STEW PIEDMONTESE

MAKES 6 SERVINGS

- 1 pound boneless pork loin, cut into 1-inch cubes
- 1 tablespoon olive oil
- 1 yellow onion, coarsely chopped
- 2 carrots, coarsely chopped
- 8 ounces mushrooms, coarsely chopped
- 1 8-ounce can tomato sauce
- 1 cup dry red wine
- 1 teaspoon dried thyme
- 1 teaspoon dried oregano
- ¼ teaspoon cinnamon
- ¼ teaspoon salt
- ½ cup raisins
- 6 cups cooked rice

Heat oil in a Dutch oven over medium heat and cook the pork until lightly browned, about 3 minutes. Add the vegetables; cook and stir 2 minutes. Add the tomato sauce, wine and seasonings. Bring to a boil; lower the heat to a simmer, cover and cook gently for 15 to 20 minutes. Stir in the raisins and heat through. Serve pork stew over hot cooked rice.

Preparation time: 15 minutes
Cooking time: 30 minutes

Pork Stew Piedmontese

CHICKEN CACCIATORE

MAKES 4 TO 6 SERVINGS

This simple recipe for "hunter's style" chicken uses bay leaves, mushrooms, wine, and dry-cured olives—typical seasonings for meat and game.

2 tablespoons olive oil
1 chicken, cut into parts
1 yellow onion, finely chopped
1 stalk celery, thinly sliced
1 clove garlic, minced
2 cups thinly sliced mushrooms
¼ cup white wine
1 8-ounce can tomato sauce
1 teaspoon dried oregano or basil
1 bay leaf
¼ cup chicken stock
  Freshly ground black pepper
  to taste
1 cup dry-cured olives

Heat olive oil in a Dutch oven over high heat. Brown the chicken a few pieces at a time. Transfer chicken to a platter. Pour off all but 2 tablespoons of oil from the pan. Add onion, celery, garlic, and mushrooms and sauté for about 5 minutes. Add the wine and let most of the liquid boil away. Return the chicken to the Dutch oven. Add the tomato sauce, oregano, bay leaf, chicken stock, black pepper, and cover. Simmer over low heat for about 30 minutes. Baste occasionally with sauce. Test for doneness by pricking the thigh with a fork; juices should run clear.

To serve, transfer the chicken pieces to a warm platter. Discard the bay leaf. Add olives to the sauce and cook for 1 to 2 minutes. Pour the sauce over the chicken.

Preparation time:
Cooking time:

STUFFED CHICKEN

MAKES 4 SERVINGS

4 chicken breasts, boned, skinned, and halved
½ cup olive oil
⅓ cup red wine vinegar
1 small head radicchio, torn into bite-sized pieces
1 small bunch watercress, cut into bite-sized pieces
¼ cup fresh basil
2 plum tomatoes, thinly sliced
1 egg
⅔ cup Italian seasoned bread crumbs
½ cup Parmesan cheese
4 tablespoons olive oil

With a meat mallet, pound the chicken to ¼-inch thickness and place in a large baking pan. Combine the olive oil and vinegar. Add ½ cup of the oil-vinegar dressing and turn to coat. Cover and refrigerate 30 minutes.

In a medium bowl, place radicchio and watercress; add the remaining ½ cup oil-vinegar dressing; toss to mix. Arrange radicchio mixture on a platter; refrigerate.

Remove chicken from the oil-vinegar dressing and drain. Cut each chicken breast half in half crosswise. Place an even portion of basil and tomatoes on each of 4 pieces of chicken. Top each piece of chicken with remaining half of breast half and, with textured side of the meat mallet, pound edges together to seal.

In a shallow dish, beat egg with 1 tablespoon of water. On wax paper, mix the bread crumbs and Parmesan cheese. Dip the chicken, one piece at a time, in the egg mixture and then in the bread crumb mixture.

Heat oil in a large frying pan on medium-high heat. Add chicken and cook about 10 minutes, or until the chicken is brown and a fork can be inserted with ease. Arrange the chicken on top of radicchio mixture.

Preparation time: 10 minutes
Chilling time: 30 minutes
Cooking time: 10 to 12 minutes

VEGETABLES
Verdure

To refer to Italy as Europe's "vegetable garden" may be pushing the truth, but not by much. Before Catherine di Medici moved to France in 1533, the rest of Europe had never even heard of such vegetables as broccoli, artichokes, and *petit pois*, the tiny peas that the French have adopted as their own. Italian cooks transformed spinach from an inconsequential side dish into an art form. The tomato may have originated in the Western Hemisphere, but it was transformed into its delicious present incarnation in Italy.

There is no household in Italy where the smell of simmering sauces and casseroles laced with garlic and made with tomatoes, eggplant, peppers, or zucchini cannot be savored.

Each region has its specialties. Ravenna produces the best asparagus, Umbria is noted for its celery and onions, and in Rome broccoli is king. The San Marzano region is known for its lovely tomatoes which are available in this country. South of Naples, it is nearly impossible to find a meal that does not include the tomato in some form.

Although eggplant is a vegetable, it almost deserves its own category under main dishes. Once known as the "love apple," there are many delicious ways to enjoy eggplant. Whether breaded, sautéed, baked, broiled, grilled, or simmered into soups or stews, it offers extraordinarily good eating. Eggplant is low in calories, virtually sodium-free and an excellent source of dietary fiber.

EGGPLANT PARMESAN

MAKES 6 TO 8 SERVINGS

2 pounds eggplant
   Salt (to sprinkle over eggplant)
2 tablespoons butter
1 cup chopped yellow onion
1 clove garlic, minced
3 tomatoes, peeled and chopped
1 6-ounce can tomato paste
¾ teaspoon dried oregano or basil
¼ teaspoon salt
2 eggs
1 cup bread crumbs
1 cup Parmesan cheese
¼ cup olive oil
¾ pound mozzarella cheese, thinly sliced

Preheat oven to 350° F. Peel the eggplant and slice into ¼-inch slices. Sprinkle with salt and drain slices in a colander for 30 minutes.

Meanwhile, prepare the sauce. Melt butter in a saucepan; sauté onion and garlic until tender. Stir in tomatoes, tomato paste, ⅓ cup of water, oregano, and salt. Simmer 10 minutes, stirring occasionally.

Squeeze out the excess moisture of the eggplant slices with a paper towel and pat dry. In a small bowl, beat eggs with 1 tablespoon of water. In another bowl, combine bread crumbs with ½ cup Parmesan cheese; mix well. Dip the eggplant slices into the egg mixture, then coat them with the crumb mixture.

Heat oil in a large skillet over medium-high heat; sauté eggplant until golden brown on both sides. Remove and drain on paper towels. Finish cooking the eggplant, adding more oil as needed.

Place enough eggplant slices to cover the bottom of an 8-inch square pan. Sprinkle with about 2 tablespoons Parmesan and ⅓ of the mozzarella. Cover with half the tomato sauce. Repeat the layers, ending with the last of the Parmesan and mozzarella cheeses. Bake for 30 minutes, or until bubbly.

Preparation time: 30 minutes
Cooking time: 40 minutes

Foreground: Eggplant Northern Style

EGGPLANT NORTHERN STYLE

MAKES 4 SERVINGS

Here baby eggplants are topped with herbed tomatoes and cheese and baked. This would also make a tasty addition to a tray of antipasto.

4	baby eggplants, or 1 large eggplant, cut in quarters
1	large clove garlic, minced
1	tablespoon olive oil
1	tablespoon chopped parsley
1/8	teaspoon crumbled oregano
1	cup Marinara Sauce (page 25)
	Salt and freshly ground black pepper
1	small tomato, diced
1 1/4	cups diced mozzarella cheese

Preheat oven to 375° F. Cut eggplants into halves lengthwise and criss-cross meaty part with a sharp knife. Place in a large skillet, add water to a depth of ½-inch, and bring to a boil. Cover and simmer 10 to 15 minutes, until eggplant is tender when pierced with a fork. Remove from pan and drain well.

Sauté garlic, cheese, parsley, and oregano. In a large baking dish, or in

four individual ones, measure about 3 to 4 tablespoons Marinara Sauce for each serving. Sprinkle eggplant lightly with salt and pepper and place skin side down in the sauce. Top with the tomato and mozzarella mixture. Bake in a moderately hot oven about 25 minutes until thoroughly heated.

Preparation time: 10 minutes
Cooking time: 45 to 50 minutes

PEPPERS PIEMONTESE
MAKES 4 SERVINGS

This lovely dish brings to mind images of the vegetable markets of the Piedmont (Piemonte) in northwest Italy with their displays of peppers—red, green and yellow—whose colors are so vivid that they scarcely appear real.

4 red bell peppers
1 clove garlic, minced
1 tablespoon olive oil
   Salt and freshly ground black
   pepper, to taste
1 tablespoon capers,
   drained and minced
3 anchovy fillets, minced
1 tablespoon red wine vinegar
   (optional)
1 lemon, cut into small wedges
1 teaspoon chopped parsley

Place peppers under broiler and broil, turning occasionally, until skins are well blistered and charred all over. Place the peppers in a small brown paper bag and twist closed. Let the peppers steam for 5 minutes. Strip off the skins by working under cold running water. Cut peppers into halves and remove seeds and cores.

In a saucepan, sauté garlic lightly in oil. Add the peppers and sauté over low heat 3 to 4 minutes, until the peppers are hot and tender. Add salt and pepper to taste and sprinkle with capers. Top with anchovies. Serve warm, or sprinkle with red wine vinegar and chill. Garnish with lemon wedges and sprinkle with chopped parsley.

Preparation time: 7 minutes
Cooking time: 5 minutes

NAVY BEANS IN WINE SAUCE
MAKES 2 QUARTS

These savory beans are the perfect accompaniment to a hearty roast or leg of lamb.

1   pound dried navy beans
2   tablespoons olive oil
¾   cup minced shallots
3   cloves garlic, minced
1   cup dry white wine
2   teaspoons salt
1   teaspoon dried rosemary leaves
1   teaspoon dried thyme leaves
1   teaspoon rubbed sage
¼   teaspoon freshly ground
     black pepper
1   14½-ounce can whole peeled
     tomatoes, drained and chopped

Rinse and clean the beans thoroughly, discarding any imperfect ones. Soak overnight in 6 cups of water.

Heat oil in a Dutch oven over medium-high heat. Sauté the shallots and garlic for 2 to 3 minutes or until the onions are tender.

Drain the navy beans and add them to the onions. Add the wine, salt, rosemary, thyme, sage, and pepper. Mix well. Add enough water to cover the beans; bring to a boil. Reduce the heat and simmer, covered for 45 minutes. Uncover and continue cooking until the beans are tender, stirring occasionally. Add more water to the beans as necessary to keep them from sticking. Add the tomatoes and cook for 15 minutes until they are heated through.

Preparation time: 10 minutes
Soaking time: Overnight
Cooking time: 2½ hours

GREEN BEANS ALLA FIORENTINA

MAKES 6 SERVINGS

1½   *pounds small, young green*
      string beans
  1   *tablespoon butter*
  ½   *clove garlic, slightly crushed*
  1   *yellow onion, coarsley chopped*
  1   *tablespoon chopped parsley*
      Freshly ground black pepper
  4   *tablespoons freshly grated*
      Parmesan cheese

Wash and remove the tips and bottoms of the green beans. Steam for 6 to 8 minutes until *al dente*. While the beans are cooking, melt the butter in a saucepan. Add the garlic and onion to the pan and sauté over medium heat until transparent. Add 5 tablespoons of water and boil for about 10 minutes or until the onion becomes soft and the water has evaporated.

Mix the drained beans with the onion, butter, and parsley. Sprinkle with pepper and cheese. Serve immediately. The beans may be placed in a hot oven or under the broiler until the cheese begins to melt.

Preparation time: 10 minutes
Cooking time: 20 minutes

BAKED ASPARAGUS

MAKES 6 TO 8 SERVINGS

12   *asparagus spears*
      Salt to taste
3½   *ounces freshly grated*
      Parmigiano-Reggiano cheese
3½   *ounces unsalted butter*
  2   *tablespoons thinly sliced Parma*
      prosciutto (optional)

Preheat the oven to 400°F. Wash and peel the lower end of the asparagus. Steam for about 4 to 6 minutes or until almost tender. Place the cooked asparagus at alternate levels in a buttered pan so that the tips are free and sprinkle grated cheese over the asparagus tips. Melt butter and pour over the asparagus. Bake until the cheese starts to melt. Garnish with Parma prosciutto.

Preparation time: 5 minutes
Cooking time: 10 to 15 minutes

BAKED SPINACH

MAKES 3 TO 4 SERVINGS

It has now been several centuries since Italian cooks transformed spinach from an inconsequential side dish into an art form, but the joy of a baked spinach casserole is still almost like a passport to the Renaissance.

  6   *eggs*
1½   *cups ricotta cheese*
  1   *tablespoon finely chopped*
      yellow onion
  2   *teaspoons flour*
  ½   *teaspoon salt*
  ½   *teaspoon dry mustard*
  1   *pound fresh spinach, cleaned,*
      chopped, cooked and well-
      drained
      Parsley (optional)

Preheat oven to 350° F. In a medium bowl, mix together all the ingredients, except spinach, until well blended. Stir in the spinach. Pour mixture into a 1½ quart casserole dish. Bake 30 to 35 minutes, or until a knife inserted near the center comes out clean. Garnish with parsley, if desired.

Preparation time: 5 minutes
Cooking time: 30 to 35 minutes

SALADS

Insalate

With an abundance of fresh vegetables available, it is easy to understand how salads (*insalate*) became an important part of Italian meal planning. During the Renaissance, salads—often involving endive and romaine lettuce—were served as a first course. Today, the salad course often follows the soup or the main course.

Salads in Italy are typically more elaborate than they are in France, where a salad might often consist simply of lettuce or endive with an oil and vinegar dressing. Pasta such as tortellini, farfelle, rotelli, and cheeses such as Fontina entered the list of ingredients for Italian salads, as did tomatoes as they became generally available in the seventeenth century.

CALAMARI SALAD

MAKES 8 TO 10 SERVINGS

5	pounds calamari, cleaned (bodies cut into rings and tentacles separated)
¾	cup olive oil
1	medium-sized bunch of parsley
5	jars (4 ounces) whole pimentos
5 to 10	cloves garlic, minced
1 to 2	cans (2 ounces each) anchovy fillets
	Worcestershire sauce
1	teaspoon Dijon-style mustard
¼	cup red wine vinegar
4	lemons
1	can medium-sized ripe olives
	Fresh parsley and lemon slices, for garnish

Place the cleaned calamari in a large skillet with its natural juices and ¼ cup olive oil. Sauté over medium heat until the calamari is barely cooked, turning frequently. Remove, drain well and let stand.

Chop the parsley and pimentos; set aside. Pour the remaining olive oil into large salad bowl and add the garlic to the oil. Add the anchovy fillets and mash well. Add 2 shakes of Worcestershire sauce and mustard. Add red wine vinegar and squeeze the juice of 2 lemons into mixture; mix well. Add the calamari, chopped parsley, pimentos, and olives. Toss well and refrigerate for at least 5 hours. Mix occasionally.

Serve the calamari salad in a decorative shallow salad bowl. Garnish with fresh parsley and slices of lemon. Just before serving, squeeze 1 or 2 additional lemons on the salad.

Preparation time: 20 minutes
Cooking time: 5 minutes
Chilling time: at least 5 hours

SALAMI AND PASTA SALAD

MAKES 2 SERVINGS

Salami and Pasta Salad

4   ounces fresh cheese tortellini, or
      2 ounces dried
4   ounces sliced salami
2   plum tomatoes, sliced
½   small green pepper, cut into thin
      strips
¼   cup thinly sliced yellow onion
1   teaspoon Dijon-style mustard
1   tablespoon olive oil
2   teaspoons red wine vinegar
      Salt and freshly ground black
      pepper, to taste

Cook the pasta 8 to 10 minutes or until *al dente*. Drain; rinse with cold water. Meanwhile, cut each slice of salami into 6 wedges and combine with tomatoes, green peppers, and onion. In a small bowl combine the mustard, oil, vinegar, salt, and pepper. Add to the salami and vegetable mixture; mix well. Add pasta to the salad and toss lightly.

Preparation time: 10 minutes
Cooking time: 8 to 10 minutes

PORK AND WILTED SPINACH SALAD

MAKES 6 SERVINGS

1   pound boneless pork loin
½   pound bacon, sliced
8   cups torn fresh spinach
¾   cup red wine vinegar
1   tablespoon sugar
      Salt to taste
1   medium apple, cored and cut
      into wedges
½   cup raisins

Slice the pork across the grain into thin strips. Cut the uncooked bacon into 1-inch pieces. In a skillet, cook the bacon till crisp; remove and drain on paper towels. Pour off the bacon drippings into a 1-cup measure, reserving 1 tablespoon of drippings in the skillet.

Add half the pork to the skillet and stir-fry for 2 to 3 minutes, until the pork is browned. Remove the cooked pork; set aside. Add the remaining pork and cook until browned.

In a large bowl combine the bacon, pork, and spinach; set aside. For the dressing, in a small saucepan combine the reserved drippings, vinegar, sugar, and salt; cook until just heated through. Pour the hot dressing over the pork-spinach salad. Add the apple and raisins and toss gently. Serve immediately.

Preparation time: 10 minutes
Cooking time: 20 minutes

SWEETS
Dolci

A traditional after-dinner dessert is a cheese and fruit tray. Typical items include Gorgonzola, mozzarella, provolone, apples, grapes, oranges, tangerines, crackers, or Italian bread sticks.

Sicilian desserts in particular are famous far beyond their native shores. Rich ricotta desserts like cannoli, ice creams, ices, sherbets, beautiful cakes, and nougats all are credited to Sicily.

TORTA DI RICOTTA

MAKES 10 TO 12 SERVINGS

One of the oldest Italian desserts, this ricotta cheese torte owes its origin to Roman bakers. Ricotta cheese is one of the most widely-used cheeses in Italian cuisine.

PASTRY

2	cups flour
½	teaspoon salt
⅔	cup shortening
1	small egg
2	tablespoons dry Marsala

Sift together flour and salt. Cut in shortening. Add egg; gradually add Marsala. Using fingertips, mix together, incorporating as much flour as possible. Form dough into a smooth ball. If necessary add enough iced water to hold ingredients together.

Roll out dough to ⅛-inch thickness and fit into a deep 10-inch pie plate. Cut remaining pastry dough into strips ½-inch wide to use as lattice top. Preheat oven to 375° F.

Preparation time: 40 minutes
Baking time: 45 minutes

FILLING

1½	pound ricotta cheese or dry cottage cheese
⅓	cup milk
¼	cup sugar
4	eggs
2	tablespoons orange flower water or almond extract
1	tablespoon grated citron, or lemon peel
½	pound blanched hazelnuts Powdered sugar

Combine ricotta, milk, and sugar; rub through a fine sieve. Beat eggs; combine with flower water or extract and lemon peel. Blend into mixture until smooth and creamy.

Pour cheese mixture on top of pastry crust. Crisscross strips of pastry over top; press edges together. Place 1 hazelnut between strips. Bake in a moderate oven for 45 minutes, or until pastry is light brown and mixture is firm but not too dry. Cool in oven with door open. Dust with powdered sugar before serving.

HAZELNUT BISCOTTI

MAKES 48 COOKIES

Biscotti, literally "twice-baked" cookies, are a little something to dunk in hot coffee, vin santo, or spumante.

1¼   cups flour
1½   teaspoons baking powder
⅛   teaspoon ground ginger
½   teaspoon salt
¼   cup butter
¾   cup sugar
¼   teaspoon vanilla extract
1   large egg
1   teaspoon grated orange peel
1   cup roasted and chopped
     hazelnuts or almonds

Preheat oven to 350° F. In a bowl, sift together the flour, baking powder, ginger, and salt; set aside.

In a another bowl, cream the butter and sugar together until light and fluffy. Beat in the vanilla, then the egg and orange peel. Add the dry ingredients and nuts and continue to mix until batter is thoroughly blended.

On a parchment-lined baking pan, form the dough into a strip roughly 3 inches wide by 12 inches long. Bake for 15 to 18 minutes. Remove from the oven and cool for 10 minutes.

Reduce the oven temperature to 300° F. Gently lift the strip from the pan and place on a cooling rack for 10 minutes. Cut the strip diagonally into ¼-inch slices. Return to the baking pan for 20 minutes, turning cookies over halfway through baking. Cool in the oven with the heat off.

Biscotti will last two weeks if stored in an airtight container.

Preparation time: 15 minutes
Cooking time: 35 to 38 minutes

PISTACHIO CAKE

MAKES 6 OR 8 SERVINGS

Pistachios are one of Italy's favorite nuts and they find their way into many dishes. This pistachio cake exemplifies the light desserts of Italy.

1   cup shelled pistachios,
     finely chopped
1   cup sugar
¾   cup butter
2   teaspoons vanilla
½   teaspoon pistachio extract or
     almond extract
3   eggs
⅔   cup unsifted flour
½   teaspoon baking powder
     Sour cream or whipped cream
     (optional)
     Ice cream (optional)
     Chocolate shavings (optional)
     Chopped pistachios (optional)

Preheat oven to 300° F. Line an 8-inch round cake pan with high sides (or a 9-inch round cake pan) with foil.

In a large bowl, combine the pistachios with sugar, butter, vanilla, and extract. Beat by hand or with a mixer until smooth and blended. Beat in eggs, one at a time. In a small bowl, mix flour with baking powder and stir it into batter.

Pour batter into the cake pan and bake until edges of cake are just beginning to pull away from the sides of the pan. The center of the cake should spring back when lightly touched. Lift cake from pan by gripping foil. Allow cake to cool. Garnish with whipped cream, chocolate shavings, and chopped pistachios.

Preparation time: 5 minutes
Cooking time: 1 hour to 1 hour 10 minutes

PANETTONE

MAKES 1 LOAF

The legendary breakfast bread of Milan, Panettone had its origin in 1490 at the dawn of the Renaissance. As the story goes, a young nobleman named Ughetto fell in love with the daughter of a baker named Antonio (Tony). His family frowned on the idea of their noble son marrying a poor baker's daughter, so the young man hatched a scheme to transform Tony into a rich baker.

It was shortly before Christmas, and all the bakers in Milan were baking their special seasonal treats. Ughetto sold his hunting falcons and used the money to buy many exotic ingredients—such as raisins and lemons—which were not then in common usage. Next, pretending to be a baker's assistant, he hired on with Tony. He then helped the baker to create a bread that was so wonderful, and so revolutionary, that people beat a path to Tony's door and his bakery flourished.

Ughetto's family was only too happy to allow him to marry the daughter of the baker who had developed the wonderful delight that came to be known as Tony's Bread—*Pane di Tony*—or Panettone.

Hardly made at home anymore, bakeries feature this sweet bread at Christmas time.

1	package (¼ ounce) active dry yeast
⅓	cup warm water, 110° F to 115° F
¼	cup sugar
6	egg yolks
1	teaspoon vanilla extract
1	teaspoon ground anise
½	teaspoon grated lemon peel
½	teaspoon salt
2 to 3	cups bread flour
½	cup butter, room temperature
⅓	cup diced candied citron or lemon peel
¼	cup golden raisins, soaked in hot water
¼	cup dark raisins, soaked in hot water
2	tablespoons chopped pine nuts or almonds
	Melted butter
	Confectioner's sugar for frosting (optional)

Dissolve the yeast in warm water in large bowl of a mixer. Sprinkle 1 teaspoon of sugar on top and let stand until bubbly, about 5 minutes. Stir in the remaining sugar, egg yolks, vanilla, anise, lemon peel, and salt. Blend in 1½ cups of flour at low speed for 30 seconds. Change to medium speed and beat for 2 minutes.

Reduce mixer to slow speed. Divide the softened butter into 3 pieces and mix one piece at a time into dough. Change beater to dough hook and add remaining flour a little at a time, or add remaining flour by hand stirring with a wooden spoon until soft dough forms. Knead on low 5 minutes or by hand 8 to 10 minutes. Toward the end of the kneading time, knead in citron, raisins, and nuts.

Put the dough in a greased bowl, turning to grease the top. Cover with plastic wrap and let rise in a warm place until doubled, about 1 hour. Punch the dough. Form the dough into a ball and place in a well-greased 3-pound coffee can. Cut a cross on the top of the ball. Cover with plastic wrap and let rise until doubled.

Remove the middle shelf of the oven and preheat to 400° F. Brush the top of the bread with melted butter. Place the can on the bottom shelf and bake 10 minutes. Reduce heat to 350° F, brush the top with more melted butter and bake 15 minutes. Brush top again with more melted butter and bake 15 to 20 minutes longer until the top is crisp and golden brown. Pierce with metal skewer; if it comes clean, the loaf is done. If the loaf tests done but the sides are not brown enough, take it out of the can and return to oven 5 to 10 minutes longer.

Place the loaf on a wire rack until cool. Frost the top with confectioner's sugar icing, if desired. Cut in thick wedges to serve.

Preparation time: 5 minutes
Baking and Rising time: 2 hours 15 minutes

At right: Panettone

RICOTTA SHORTCAKE RING WITH VERY BERRY CHERRY SAUCE

MAKES 8 TO 10 SERVINGS

Sweeten any fresh fruit of the season to serve with this shortcake. Individual shortcakes may be dropped onto a baking sheet and baked for 12 to 15 minutes. The shortcake ring can be made in advance and frozen.

SAUCE

- 1 pint strawberries, cleaned, hulled, and halved
- ½ pint raspberries
- 2 cups pitted sweet cherries
- ¾ cup sugar, or to desired sweetness
- 3 tablespoons kirsch, or another liqueur (optional)

SHORTCAKE

- 2 cups all-purpose flour
- 1 tablespoon baking powder
- 2 tablespoons sugar
- ½ teaspoon salt
- 6 tablespoons unsalted butter, cut into pieces
- 1 cup ricotta cheese or dry cottage cheese
- ⅔ cup milk
- 1 tablespoon sugar
   Sweetened whipped cream for garnish

Preheat oven to 425° F. Combine the fruits in a bowl. Toss with sugar and liqueur; set aside. Stir occasionally.

Sift the flour, baking powder, sugar, and salt together. Place the flour mixture in a blender or food processor and whirl together 3 to 4 times. Add the ricotta cheese; whirl 5 to 6 times to crumble together. With the blender or processor running, slowly add milk. Process about 5 seconds until all ingredients are well mixed.

Turn out the dough onto the center of a baking sheet. Smooth the dough into an 8-inch flat circle. Form a 3-inch hole in the center of the dough, making a ring 2½ inches thick. Sprinkle the surface of the ring with 1 tablespoon sugar. Bake for 20 to 25 minutes. Cool on the baking sheet 20 minutes, then remove to a wire rack.

Just before serving, slice the shortcake in half horizontally with a serrated knife. Remove the top. Place the bottom on a large serving platter. Top with half the fruit. Placed the top of the shortcake over the fruit. Top with the remaining fruit. Garnish with whipped cream.

Preparation time: 30 minutes
Cooking time: 20 to 25 minutes

LEMON ICE

MAKES 4 SERVINGS

- 3 cups water
- 2 cups sugar
- 1 cup fresh lemon juice

Boil water and sugar together for 5 minutes. Remove from heat. Add lemon juice; mix well. Pour into an ice tray and freeze until firm, stirring occasionally.

Preparation time: 5 minutes
Cooking time: 5 minutes
Freezing time: 2 to 3 hours

CHOCOLATE GELATO

MAKES 8 TO 10 SERVINGS

Gelato is a creamy, sweet ice cream that is often served in fresh waffle cones from street vendors.

½   pound bitter chocolate
3   eggs, well beaten
½   cup sugar
1   quart milk
1   tablespoon almond extract

Set the freezer control to the coldest setting.

Melt the chocolate in the top of a double boiler. Add eggs, sugar, milk, and blend well with whisk. Continue cooking over low heat, stirring constantly, for about 8 minutes or until mixture comes to a boil. Boil 2 minutes. Add almond extract. Remove from heat and beat with a rotary beater. Cool.

Pour mixture into freezing trays and spread evenly. Freeze until firm but not frozen. Transfer to a chilled bowl and beat until smooth and creamy. Return mixture to trays and freeze until firm, stirring occasionally. When ice cream is frozen, wrap in aluminum foil to prevent ice crystals from forming.

Preparation time: 10 minutes
Cooking time: 20 to 30 minutes
Freezing time: 2 to 3 hours

TIRAMI SU

MAKES 8 TO 10 SERVINGS

Tirami su, which means "pick me up," is a traditional Venetian dessert. This recipe incorporates the customary espresso, chocolate, grappa, and mascarpone.

1   cup crushed Italian hazelnut
    biscotti (about 16 cookies)
    (page 55)
3   tablespoons Italian grappa
    (distilled liquor)
2   ounces semi-sweet chocolate,
    cut into small pieces
1   tablespoon instant espresso
    crystals
1   cup milk
3   egg yolks
⅓   cup sugar
1   envelope (3 ounces) unflavored
    gelatin
3   tablespoons cold milk
1   pound mascarpone cheese
    Whipped cream
    Chocolate shavings

In a small bowl, combine the crushed cookies and grappa; set aside.

In a medium saucepan, combine the chocolate pieces, espresso crystals, and milk. Cook over medium-low heat, stirring constantly, until hot. Do not boil. Set aside.

In a medium mixing bowl, beat the egg yolks and sugar with an electric mixer until very light in color. Add the hot milk mixture; stir. Return to the pan. Whisk constantly over medium-low heat until frothing subsides and the mixture is thickened, about 10 to 12 minutes. Do not boil.

Soften the gelatin in 3 tablespoons of cold milk. Add the softened gelatin to the hot mixture and stir until completely dissolved. Pour into a medium bowl. Set aside to cool, stirring occasionally.

When completely cool but not set, beat the mixture into the mascarpone cheese with an electric mixer. Stir in the crushed cookies. Rinse a 4 to 5 cup mold with cold water and pour the mixture into it. Cover and refrigerate for at least 12 hours.

To unmold, set the mold in a basin of hot water for 1 to 2 seconds. Invert onto a serving platter. Garnish with whipped cream and chocolate shavings.

Preparation time: 15 minutes
Cooking time: 15 minutes
Chilling time: 12 hours

NUTRITION AND THE ITALIAN KITCHEN

Italians have known for centuries that the way to a healthy heart is through the stomach, and their diet reflects this. By cooking in olive oil and herbs, eating fresh vegetables, pastas, and small portions of meats that have been cooked without added fats, drinking a little wine, and having the biggest meal at midday, Italians keep the body healthy and well-fed.

Major health organizations recommend balancing daily caloric intake between 55 percent carbohydrates, 15 percent protein and 30 percent fat. Balancing the type of fat you eat is important, too: No more than 10 percent of a day's total fat intake should come from saturated fats. For example, a 2000 calorie daily diet could contain up to 67 grams total fat (30 percent of calories) and 22 grams of saturated fat (10 percent of calories).

By cooking foods yourself, you have more control over what you eat. There are a few simple guidelines you can follow to help control fat and calories in meat selection:

◆ Choose lean meat cuts. As a rule of thumb, beef cuts with *loin* or *round* in the name, and pork, veal, and lamb cuts with *loin* or *leg* in the name are the leanest choices. Choose ground meat products that are 80 to 90 percent lean. Buy lean deli meats.

◆ Trim all visible fat from meat before cooking and eating.

◆ Use cooking methods that reduce rather than add fat. Broil and roast on a rack, panbroil, grill or microwave. These cooking methods require no additional fat. Remove fat from soups, stews and casseroles by chilling them and skimming the hardened fat from the top. Tenderize lean cuts by cooking slowly with moist heat, cooking in liquid or marinating. Pounding, grinding, and slicing across the grain also helps.

Having two or three servings per day of lean meat, poultry, dry beans, and eggs, with a daily total of about 6 ounces, fits easily into the recommended fat intake for one day. Four ounces of boneless raw meat will equal about 3 ounces cooked. A 3-ounce cooked, trimmed serving of beef, pork, veal, or lamb is about the size of a deck of cards.

Eat foods rich in complex carbohydrates like whole grain breads and cereals, pasta, rice, dried peas and beans, and fruits and vegetables. If eaten plain, they are low in fat and are good sources of vitamins, minerals, and fiber. Remembering the importance of the total diet over time and planning meals with daily caloric intake in mind is one of the best ways to control hidden fat and establish overall good health.

Sometimes foods that claim to be "cholesterol-free" or "low-cholesterol" may contian large amounts of hidden fat, including saturated fat. In order to prevent being misled, read the nutrition label to learn the amount of total fat, saturated fat, and cholesterol in a serving. Learn where hidden fats lie and become familiar with the composition of favorite foods.

Saturated fat raises blood cholesterol more than anything else in the diet, even more than dietary cholesterol. So one of the goals in a blood cholesterol-lowering diet is to eat less saturated fat. Saturated fat and foods that are high in saturated fat usually are solid at room temperature. They include butter, cheese, and meat. (Whole milk, which has a relatively high saturated fat content is one exception to this general rule.)

Unsaturated fats (polyunsaturated and monounsaturated) are healthy substitutes for saturated fat. Vegetable oils such as safflower, corn, soybean, cottonseed, sesame, and sunflower oils are good sources of polyunsaturated fats. However, a few vegetable oils also are naturally high in saturated fat—coconut oil and palm kernel oil. (Consumption of these oils accounts for about 4 percent of the fat in the U.S. diet.) Fish also contains polyunsaturated fats. Olive, peanut, and canola oil are high in monounsaturated fats.

Cholesterol is found only in food from animal sources, such as egg yolks, dairy products, meat, poultry, shellfish, and—in smaller amounts—fish. Also, organ meats—liver or kidney for instance—are particularly rich in cholesterol.

Sodium is found in salt (sodium chloride). High blood pressure—a major risk factor for heart attack, stroke, and kidney disease in some people—is sometimes associated with a diet that is high in sodium. The best approach is to limit daily sodium intake to less than 3000 milligrams.

Excerpted from *FDA Consumer*, March 1989, *The Official Magazine of the U.S. Food and Drug Administration*; and *Nutrition Strategies: Designs for Heart-Healthy Living* produced by the National Live Stock and Meat Board, Beef Promotion and Research Board, and National Pork Board, 1990.

THE WINES OF ITALY

The ancient Greeks referred to Italy as Oenotria, the land of wine. In this regard, nothing has changed.

The enjoyment of wine is widespread in Italy, indeed there are few places on the peninsula where vineyards do not flourish. Each hillside in Italy has its own personality that lends itself to the wine produced there. The soil, climate, vine varieties, vineyard maintenance, winemakers' technique and ageing all affect the outcome of a wine.

There are 232 wine-producing zones in Italy that are classified as regions of the highest quality or denominazione di origine controllata (DOC) and six DOCG (the "G" for garantita or guaranteed), areas that are the equivalent of the appellation contrôlée in France. While only 10 to 12 percent of Italy's wine production is classified, the DOC/DOCG output is 7 million hectoliters of wine per year, more than most countries produce in total.

One typically associates red wines with Italy, because they have built a reputation abroad; the most respected are the noble reds, exemplified by Barolo, Barbaresco, Brunello, and reserve Chianti. But in truth, Italy produces a full range of wines with sweet and dry varieties of white (vino bianco), rosé (vino rosato) and red (vino rosso). Italian wines in special categories include sparkling wines (vino spumante), light bubbly wines (vino frizzante), and new wines (vino novelli).

The heart of the Chianti region lies between Florence and Sienna in the province of Tuscany and is known for Chianti Classico (a historical area), the deep red, dry wine with a rich, full flavor. To the south, Apulia (Puglia) in the heel of the boot, produces distinguished red wines, as do Campania and

A vineyard in the Chianti region

Sicily in the deep south. In the Alpine foothills of the north surrounding Piedmont, a good portion of the acreage is planted in vineyards. Piedmont is well known for Barolo and Barbaresco as well as for Asti Spumante and vermouth.

White wine is produced throughout Italy, with the most popular being Soave, a pale, dry type from the Veneto region around Verona and Lake Garda. Trentino-Alto Adige, the formerly Austrian region around Bolzano (in German, Bozen) is known for its white wines that resemble the whites of its neighbor Germany. Tuscany also produces a well-known va-

rietal white wine known as Trebbiano. However, its most important white is Vernaccia di San Gimignano. In the sun-washed hills between Tuscany and Rome, one finds other excellent wines. Orvieto in Umbria is the home of white and rosé wines, and wines that are both dry and sweet. Latium produces

Frascati. The Marches on the Adriatic Sea also boasts a white wine called Verdicchio dei Castelli di Jesi that complements the regional fish and seafood dishes.

Both the Italian sparkling wines and the vini novelli have recently gained popularity abroad. Most sparkling wine is made in the north, in the Tre Venezie, Lombardy, and Piedmont. The vini novelli are found in Tuscany and the Tre Venezie. Emilia-Romagna is a major producer of lightly bubbly wines, both Red Lambrusco and whites.

Many fine Italian wines are available in North America.

GLOSSARY

ACCIUGHE (ahk-CHOO-gay): anchovies

ACETO (ah-CHEH-toh): vinegar

AFFUMICATO (ahf-foo-mee-KAH-toh): smoked or cured

AGLIO (AH-l'yo): garlic

AGNELLO (ah-N'YEHL-lo): lamb that has been weaned

AGNOLOTTI (ah-n'yo-LOHT-tee): literally, "little fat lambs;" crescent-shaped pasta similar to ravioli with meat filling

AL DENTE (AHL-den-teh): literally "to the tooth," a term used to describe the ideal consistency of properly-cooked pasta; slightly underdone to American pallets; firm and resistant

AL FORNO (ahl-FOR-no): baked

ANTIPASTO (ahn-tee-PAHS-toh): literally "before the meal"—hors d'oeuvre, or a first course

ARISTA (ah-REE-stah): roasted loin of pork

ASPARAGI (ah-SPAR-ah-jee): asparagus

ASTI SPUMANTE (AH-stee spoo-MAHN-teh): sparkling white wine from the Piedmont

ARROSTO (ah-ROH-sto): a roast of meat

ASIAGO (ah-zee-Y'AH-go): Italian-style cheese; also made in Wisconsin; semisoft, buttery when mild; ripens with age; becomes harder in texture and sharper, fuller, and richer in flavor

BASILICO (bah-ZEE-lee-ko): basil

BEL PAESE (BEL PAH-ey-zay): soft, ripened, mild cheese with a creamy texture; originated in Lombardy

BISCOTTI (bee-SKOT-tee): literally, "twice baked;" cookies or biscuits

BISTECCA (bee-STEHK-kah): beef or veal steak

BRACIOLA (brah-CHOH-lah): cutlet or steak

BUE (BOO-eh): beef

BURRO (BOOR-ro): butter

CACCIATORE (kah-chah-TOR-reh): "hunter's style;" meat or fish cooked in a sauce that includes tomatoes, scallions, mushrooms, bay leaves, and red or white wine

CAFFE ESPRESSO (kahf-FEH-ess-PRESS-so): strong, black coffee made by forcing steam through finely ground, dark roasted coffee

CAFFELATTE (kahf-feh-LAT-teh): an espresso drink of equal parts coffee and steamed milk

CALAMARI (kah-lah-MA-ree), **CALAMARETTI** (kah-lah-ma-RET-tee): squid, tiny squid

CALDO, MOLTO CALDO (MOHL-toh KAHL-doh): warm, hot

CANNELLONI (kah-nay-LOE-nee): usually flat squares of pasta rolled around a stuffing to form tubular pasta; literally "large reeds"

CANNOLI (kah-NO-lee): tubes of crips pastry filled with ricotta cheese, chocolate, and candied fruit

CAPPELLETTI (kahp-pay-LEH-tee): moist, stuffed pasta usually served in soup; literally "little hats"

CAPPERI (kahp-PEH-ree): capers

CAPPUCCINO (kahp-poo-CHEE-no): an espresso drink of coffee topped with a thin layer of steamed milk foam

CARCIOFI (kahr-CHAW-fee): artichokes

CARNE (KAR-neh): meat

CAROTE (KAH-raw-teh): carrots

CEDRO (CHEH-d'roh): citron

CECI (CHEH-chee): garbanzo beans, chick-peas

CHIANTI (kee-YAN-tee): a dry, red wine

CIOCCOLATO (chee'yoh-ko-LA-toh): chocolate

CIPOLLA (chee-POHL-lah): onion

CONCHIGLIETTE (cone-keel-YAY-tay): pasta shaped like little sea shells; sometimes called "maruzzelle"

CONTORNI (kohn-TOR-nee): vegetables accompanying the main course, or garnishes

COSCETTO (kohs-CHET-toh), **COSCIOTTO** (kohs-CHOH-toh): leg of lamb

COSTOLETTA (kohs-toh-LET-tah), **COTOLETTA** (ko-toh-LET-tah): chop or cutlet

COTTO (KOT-toh): cooked, done

CROSTA (KROHS-tah), **CROSTATA** (krohs-TAH-tah), **CROSTATINA** (krohs-tah-TEE-nah): crust, pie crust, tart

CROSTINI (krohs-TEE-nee): crouton, or a small piece of toast garnished and served as an appetizer

DOLCI (dohl-CHEE): sweets; cakes

ERBA (ehr-BAH): herb

FAGIOLI (fah-JOE-lee): dried kidney beans

FAGIOLINI (fah-joe-LEE-nee): string beans, French beans

FARCITO (far-CHEE-toh): stuffed

FARFALLE (far-FAHL-lee): pasta shaped into small and large ribbon bows

FARINA (far-REE-nah): flour

FETTUCCINE (feh-too-CHEE-neh): noodles about ¼-inch wide

FONDI DI CARCIOFO (FOHN-dee-dee kar-CHOH-fo): artichoke hearts

FONTINA (fohn-TEE-nah): cheese of Italian origin available in the United States, made with fresh whole milk; from semisoft to hard

FORMAGGIO (fohr-MAH-jo): cheese

FORNO, AL FORNO (FOHR-no, ahl FOHR-no): baked

FREDDO (FRED-doh): cold

FRESCO (FRESS-ko): fresh, uncooked

FRITTATA (free-TAH-tah): omelet

FRUTTA (FROO-tah): fruit

FRUTTI DI MARE (FROO-tee dee MAH-reh): "fruit of the sea;" an assortment of shellfish

FUNGHI (FOON-ghee): mushrooms

FUSILLI (foo-SEE-lee): a spiraled, curly spaghetti

GAMBERETTI (gahm-beh-RET-tee): small shrimp

GAMBERI (GAHM-beh-ree): shrimp

GELATO (jeh-LAH-toh): frozen; refers to ice cream or sherbert

GORGONZOLA (gor-gahn-ZOH-lah): very pungent, highly flavored, creamy-white cheese flaked with green mold, as is Roquefort cheese; from Lombardy

GRANITE (grah-NEE-teh): Italian flavored ices

GRAPPA (GRAHP-pah): brandy made by fermenting the pressings of grapes after the juice, or must, has been drawn off

GRISSINI (gree-SEE-nee): bread sticks

IMPANATO (im-pah-NAH-toh): breaded

IMBOTTITO (im-boht-TEE-toh): stuffed

INSALATA (een-sah-LAH-tah): salad

INSALATA MISTA (een-sah-LAH-tah MEE-stah): mixed salad

LARDO AFFUMICATO (LAR-doh ahf-foo-mee-KAH-toh): bacon

LASAGNA (lah-ZAHN-n'yah): broad, flat noodles about 1½-inches wide

LATTE (LAH-teh): milk

LATTUGA (laht-TOO-gah): lettuce

LAURO (la'OO-ro): bay leaf

LEGUME (leh-GOO-meh): vegetable

LIMONE (lee-MOH-neh): lemon

LINGUINE (leen-G'WEE-nee): narrow, plain noodles about ⅛-inch wide

LUMACHINE (loo-mah-KEE-neh): small, snail-shaped pasta

MACCHERONI (mah-kay-ROE-nee): macaroni

MAGGIORANA (mah-joh-RAH-nah): marjoram

MAIALE (mah-YAH-leh): pork

MANDORLE (MAHN-dor-leh): almonds

MANICOTTI (mah-nee-KAW-tee): large rectangles of pasta dough rolled around a stuffing; also, large pasta tubes, about 4 inches long and 1 inch in diameter

(ALLA) MARINARA ([AHL-lah] mah-ree-NAH-rah): "sailor style;" sauce used in southern Italian cooking, including tomato, garlic, oil, oregano

MARINATO (mah-re-NAH-toh): marinated

MARSALA (mahr-SAHL-ah): fortified, amber-colored wine; either dry or sweet

MELANZANA (may-lahn-ZAH-nah): eggplant

MELE (MAY-lay): apples

MINESTRA (mee-NEH-strah), **MINESTRE** (mee-NEH-streh): soup or pasta course

MINESTRONE (mee-nes-TROE-neh): thick vegetable soup; sometimes contains meat

MORTADELLA (mor-tah-DEL-lah): large spiced pork sausage

MOSTACCIOLI (moe-stah-CHAW-lee): hollow, tubular pasta cut obliquely, about 2½ inches long

MOZZARELLA (mod-dzah-REL-lah): a smooth, moist, white unsalted cheese with a delicate flavor, characterized by it's stringy texture when cooked; originally made from full-cream buffalo milk, but then "Fior di Latte" (top of the milk) mozzarella produced from cow's milk became popular

NOCE MOSCATA (NOH-che-moh-SKAH-tah): nutmeg

OLIO (OH-l'yo): oil

ORIGANO (oh-REE-gah-no): wild marjoram, oregano

PANE (PAH-neh): bread

PANETTONE (pah-nay-TOE-nay): Christmas fruit bread

PANNA (PAHN-nah): cream

PANNA MONTATA (PAHN-nah mohn-TAH-tah): whipped cream

PARMIGIANO (par-mee-JAH-no): also called *formaggio di grana* (for-MAH-jo dee GRAH-nah) cheese made from part skim milk with a lower moisture and butterfat content; a yellow, mild, dry cheese known as "Parmesan;" sweet, buttery, nutty flavor; when young it is an excellent slicing cheese; when aged it's a hard (or grana) cheese that can be grated

PASTA (Pah-stah): basically a dough of flour and water used to make noodles; generic name for pasta products, from spaghetti to cannelloni

PASTICCERIA (pah-stik-CHEH-ree-yah): pastry

PASTINA (pah-STEE-nah): tiny pasta used only in soups

PATATA (pah-tah-tah): potato

PENNE (PEHN-neh): smooth, tubular, very hollow pasta, cut obliquely in 2½-inch lengths, about ½-inch in diameter

PEPE NERO (PEH-peh NEH-ro), **PEPE ROSSO** (PEh-peh ROHS-so): black pepper, red pepper

PEPERONI (peh-peh-RO-nee): green peppers or red sweet peppers (pimento); also, in the United States only, a spicy sausage

PEPERONCINI (peh-peh-rohn-CHEE-nee): dried or fresh hot red peppers

PESCE (PEHS-cheh): fish

PESTO (PEHS-toh): paste of fresh basil, Parmesan cheese, garlic, and thinned with olive oil, served in soup or over pasta; a specialty of Genoa

PIGNOLI (peen-YAW-lee): pine nuts

PISELLI (pee-ZEL-lee): peas

POLENTA (poe-LEN-tah): cornmeal mush

POLLO (PAWL-loh): chicken

POLPETTE (poel-PEHT-teh): meatballs

POMODORO (po-mo-DOH-ro); tomato

PORCHETTA (pohr-KEHT-tah): roasted whole suckling pig

PREZZEMOLO (pred-DZEH-mo-lo): parsley

PROSCIUTTO (pro-SHOO-toh): dry-cured ham usually served in thin slices

PROVOLONE (pro-vo-LOHN-neh): a creamy white cheese in appearance, with a mild to piquant flavor depending on its age; rather hard, slicing cheese; molded into small balls and sold with a wax covering

RAGU (rah-GOO): meat sauce, stew

RAVIOLI (rah-vee-Y'OHL-lee): freshly prepared, moist, very thin pasta, about 2 inches square; filled with chopped meat, spinach, and ricotta

RICOTTA (ree-KOHT-tah): a fresh, moist, unsalted cottage cheese for cooking and pastries; used very much like cream cheese in sandwiches and salads

RIGATONI (ree-gah-TOHN-nee): large, ribbed, tubular pasta cut into 3-inch lengths

RIPIENO (ree-PYAY-noh): stuffed

RISO (REE-zoe): rice

RISOTTO (ree-ZAW-Toh): rice mixture

ROMANO (roh-MAHN-no): hard grating cheese similar to Parmesan but with a fuller flavor

ROSMARINO rohz-mah-REE-no): rosemary

SALAME (sah-LAH-meh): salami

SALE (SAH-leh): salt

SALSA (SAHL-sah): sauce

SALSICCIA (sahl-SEE-chah): sausage

SALTARE (sahl-TAH-reh): sauté

SALVIA (SAHL-v'yah): sage

SCALOPPINE (skahl-oh-PEE-neh): thin slice, usually veal

SCAMPI (SKAHM-pee): a type of shrimp native to the Adriatic Sea

SEDANO (SEH-dah-no): celery

SEMIFREDDO (SEH-mee-FREH-do): mousse, chilled pudding

SEMOLINO (SAY-MOH-lee-no): a coarse meal made from wheat

SPAGHETTI (spah-GHET-tee): a wheat-flour pasta dried in long, thin, tubular lengths

SPAGHETTINI (spah-ghet-TEE-nee): very thin spaghetti; not quite as slender as vermicelli

SPINACI (spee-NAH-chee): spinach

SPUMANTE (spoo-MAHN-teh): generic term for sparkling wines (e.g., Asti Spumante, Lambrusco)

SPUMONE (spoo-MO-neh): light, foamy ice cream made with egg whites or whipped cream

TACCHINO (tahk-KEE-no): turkey

TAGLIATELLE (tahl-yay-TEL-leh): a flat pasta about ¾-inch wide

TALEGGIO (tah-LEH-jo): surface ripened, whole-milk cheese with creamy, smooth texture; originally made in the Taleggio Valley in Lombardy; good as a dessert cheese

TARTUFI (tar-TOO-fee): truffles

TIMO (TEE-mo): thyme

TONNO (TOHN-no): tuna fish

TORRONE (tohr-RO-neh): nougat

TORTA (TAWR-tah): cake, tart, pie

TORTELLINI (tohr-teh-LEE-nee): freshly prepared moist pasta shaped like "little hats;" usually filled with chopped meat or ham and cheese

UOVO (WO-vo): egg; **TUORLA D'UOVO** (TWOR-lo DWO-vo): egg yolk; **BIANCO D'UOVO** (BY-AHN-ko DWO-vo): egg white

UVA (oo-vah): grapes

UVA PASSA (OO-vah PAHS-sah): raisins

VERMICELLI (verh-mee-CHEL-lee): angel hair, very thin spaghetti; usually dried separately like spaghetti; however, sometimes 15 or 20 strands are twisted to resemble a bowknot

VINO (VEE-no): wine

VITELLO (vee-TEH-loh), **VITELLONE** (vee-tel-LO-neh): veal, calf

VONGOLE (VAWN-go-leh): clams

ZAFFERANO (dzahf-feh-RAH-no): saffron

ZUCCHINI (zoo-KEE-nee): slender, green, summer squash about 5 inches long

ZUCCHERO (DZOO-kek-ro): sugar

ZUPPA (ZOO-pah): soup

INDEX

Abruzzi 9, 14, 38
Adriatic Sea 9, 34
Africa 6, 38
Alto Adige 9
Antipasti see Appetizers
Apulia 9, 22, 61
Appetizers 10-15, 49, 62
　Antipasto 49, 62
　Antipasto Platter 10, 16
　Bagna Cauda 13
　Basic Bruschetta 14, 15
　Frittata 62
　Herb-Marinated Mushrooms 12
　Pesto Spread 11
　Pesto Topping 15, 5
　Pizza Frittata 13
　Roasted Garlic 12
　Tuscan Topping 14, 15
Arezzo 35
Austria 9
Balsamic vinegar 8
Barbaresco see Wines
Barolo see Wines
Basil 8, 24, 62
Basilicata 9
Bologna 7, 9, 38
Breads 13, 14, 23, 54, 56, 57, 60
　Breadsticks 13, 23, 54
　Garlic Bread 14
　Panettone 56, 57
Butter 8, 36
　Lemon-Garlic Butter 36
Cakes 54, 55, 58
　Pistachio Cake 55
　Ricotta Shortcake 58
　Torta di Ricotta 54
Calabria 9, 30, 38
Calamari 34, 36-37, 62
　Calamari Festival Style 37
　Deep-Fried Calamari 36
　How To Clean Calamari 37
Calzone 22
Campania 9
Cannoli see Sweets
Capocolla 38
Carne see Meats
Cheeses 8, 18, 24, 54, 63 see also Nutrition
　Asiago 33
　Fontina 52
　Gorgonzola 10, 54
　Mozzarella 8, 10, 54, 63
　Parmagiano Reggiano 8, 18, 24, 63
　Provolone 10, 54
　Ricotta 8, 54, 63
Chianti see Wines
China 6
Corsica 9
Cortez 6
Croatia 9
Desserts see Sweets
Dolci see Sweets
Doughs 20, 23, 24, 25, 26, 31
　Breadsticks 23
　Homemade Pasta Dough 25, 26
　Homemade Pizza Dough 20
　Ravioli 24, 31
Eggplant 19, 48, 49
　Creamy Eggplant Soup 19
　Eggplant Northern Style 49, 49
　Eggplant Parmesan 48
Emilia-Romagna 9, 18, 38, 61
England 6
Florence 6, 9, 38

France 6, 9, 48
Fruit 54
Frutti di Mare see Seafood
Garlic 8, 9, 12, 13, 14, 24
　Bagna Cauda 13
　Garlic Bread 14
　Garlic Press 9
　Roasted Garlic 12
Gulf of Taranto 34
Ice cream 59
　Chocolate Gelato 59
Insalate see Salads
Lamb 43, 44, 50, 60
　Lamb Kebobs 43
　Loin Lamb Chops Romana 44
　Roast Leg Of Lamb 44, 50
Lasagna 28, 62
Latium 9, 61
Liguria 7, 9, 42
Ligurian Sea 9, 34
Linguine 14, 27, 62
Lombardy 9
Manicotti 31, 63
Marches, The 9, 38, 61
Meats 10, 18, 39-46 see also Nutrition
　Capocollo 10
　Lamb Kebobs 43
　Lean Homemade Sausage 46
　Loin Lamb Chops Romana 44
　Meatballs In A Basket 40
　Osso Buco 41
　Poached Beef Rib Eye Roast 39, 39
　Pork With Artichokes And Capers 45
　Pork Stew Piedmontese 46, 46
　Prosciutto 10, 18
　Roast Leg Of Lamb 44
　Salami 10, 38
　Soprassoto 38
　Steak And Spaghetti Squash 40
　Stuffed Pork Loin Genovese 45
　Veal Marsala 41
　Veal Piccata 42
　Veal Tonnato 43
Medici, Catherine di 6, 48
Mediterranean Sea 6, 9, 34
Mexico 6
Milan 56
Minestrone see Soups
Molise 38
Mostaccioli 29, 63
Mozzarella see Cheeses
Mushrooms 10, 47
Naples 6, 7, 9, 18, 22, 48
Nutrition 60
Olives 10, 22, 47
　Dry-cured olives 10, 47
Olive oil 8, 14, 24, 60
Oregano 8, 16
Pancetta 8
Pane see Breads
Parmesan see Cheeses
Parmigiano-Reggiano (Parmesan) 8, 18, 24, 63
Pasta 6, 7, 24-32, 38, 60, 63
　Capellini 24
　Farfelle 24, 52
　Fettuccine 24
　Hazelnut Manicotti 31
　Homemade Pasta 26
　Lasagna 24, 28, 29

Linguine With Garlic Clam Sauce 27
Linguine With Italian Sausage 27
Maccheroni 24
Mostaccioli With Meat Sauce 29
Pasta Primavera With Rotelli 30
Penne 24, 30
Penne Arrabbiata 30
Ravioli 24, 31
Ruote 24
Rotelli 30, 52
Spaghetti Alla Carbonara 26
Tortellini 24
Vermicelli 24
Peppers Piemontese 50
Persia 6
Pesto 11, 15, 24
　Pesto Sauce 24
　Pesto Spread 11
　Pesto Topping 15
Piedmonte 9, 50, 61
Pizza 20-23
　Four Cheese Pizza 21
　Homemade Pizza Dough 20
　Pizza Maargherita 20, 21, 23
　Sausage Pizza 22
Polenta 24, 33
　Baked Polenta With Asiago And Mushroom Sauce 33
Pollame see Poultry
Polo, Marco 6
Pork 38, 45, 46, 60
　Porchetta 38
　Pork With Artichokes And Capers 45
　Pork Stew Piedmontese 46, 46
　Stuffed Pork Loin Genovese 45
Poultry 47 see also Nutrition
　Chicken Cacciatore 47
　Stuffed Chicken 47
Provolone see Cheeses
Ravenna 48
Ravioli 31, 63
Red Pepper 27
Renaissance 6
Rice 24, 32, 33, 41, 60
　Arborio rice 24
　Risotto Alla Milanese 33, 41
　Risotto With Peas And Mushrooms 32, 32
Ricotta see Cheeses
Riso see Rice
Romano see Cheeses
Rome 6, 9, 48, 61
Romans 38
Rosemary 8
Rotelli 30
Salads 52-53
　Calamari Salad 52
　Pork And Wilted Spinach Salad 53
　Salami And Pasta Salad 53, 53
San Marzano 48
Sardinia 9, 24
Sauces 24, 25, 27, 33, 37, 41, 43, 58, 63
　Alfredo 24
　Béchamel 6
　Berry Cherry Sauce 58
　Bolognese 24
　Burro 24
　Garlic Clam Sauce 27
　Marinara Sauce 25, 63

Meat Sauce 29
Mushroom Sauce 33
Pesto Sauce 24
Pizzaiola 24
Pomodoro 24
Red Sauce 37
Tonnato Sauce 43
Verde 24
Vongole 24
Sausages 38
　Lean Homemade Sausage 46
　Salami 38
　Sausage Pizza 22
　Soprassoto 38
Seafood 10, 13, 34-38
　Anchovies 10, 13, 34
　Calamari 34, 62
　Calamari Festival Style 37
　Clams 34
　Deep-Fried Calamari 36
　Mussels 34
　Oysters 34, 38
　Sardines 10
　Scampi 34
　Sea bass 34
　Seafood Stew 34
　Shrimp 34
　Sole 34
　Tuna 10, 34, 43
Sicily 9, 24, 61
Sienna 32
Spaghetti 26, 63
Spain 6
Soave see Wines
Soups 16-19, 63
　Beef Minestrone Soup 16, 17
　Creamy Eggplant Soup 19
　Pasta And Chickpea Soup 18
　Tortellini Soup 19, 63
Spumante see Wines
Squid see Calamari
Sweets 54-59
　Chocolate Gelato 59
　Hazelnut Biscotti 55
　Lemon Ice 58
　Panettone 56, 57, 63
　Pistachio Cake 55
　Ricotta Shortcake Ring With Very Berry Cherry Sauce 58, 63
　Tirami Su 59
　Torta Di Ricotta 54
Switzerland 9
Tomatoes 8
Tuscan Topping 14
Tuscany 7, 9, 38, 61
Umbria 9, 48, 61
Utensils 9
Valle d'Aosta 9
Veal 38, 41-43, 60
　Osso Buco 41
　Veal Marsala 41
　Veal Piccata 42, 42
　Veal Saltimbocca 38
　Veal Tonnato 43
Vegetables 48-51
　Baked Asparagus 51
　Baked Spinach 51
　Eggplant Northern Style 49, 49
　Eggplant Parmesan 48
　Green Beans Alla Fiorentina 51
　Navy Beans In Wine Sauce 50
　Peppers Piemontese 50

Venice 6, 7, 9
Veneto 9
Verdure see Vegetables
Wild game 38
Wine 27, 41, 47, 61, 61
Zuppe see Soups

PHOTO CREDITS
California Beef Council 17
Florida Tomato Committee 3, 21
Fresh Garlic Association 49
© Ming Photography 57
National Broiler Council 29
National Live Stock and Meat Board 11, 39, 42, 53
National Pork Producers Council 46
USA Rice Council 32
Wheat Foods Council 25
Wisconsin Milk Marketing Board 15
© Bill Yenne 2, 7, 32, 35, 38, 42, 61

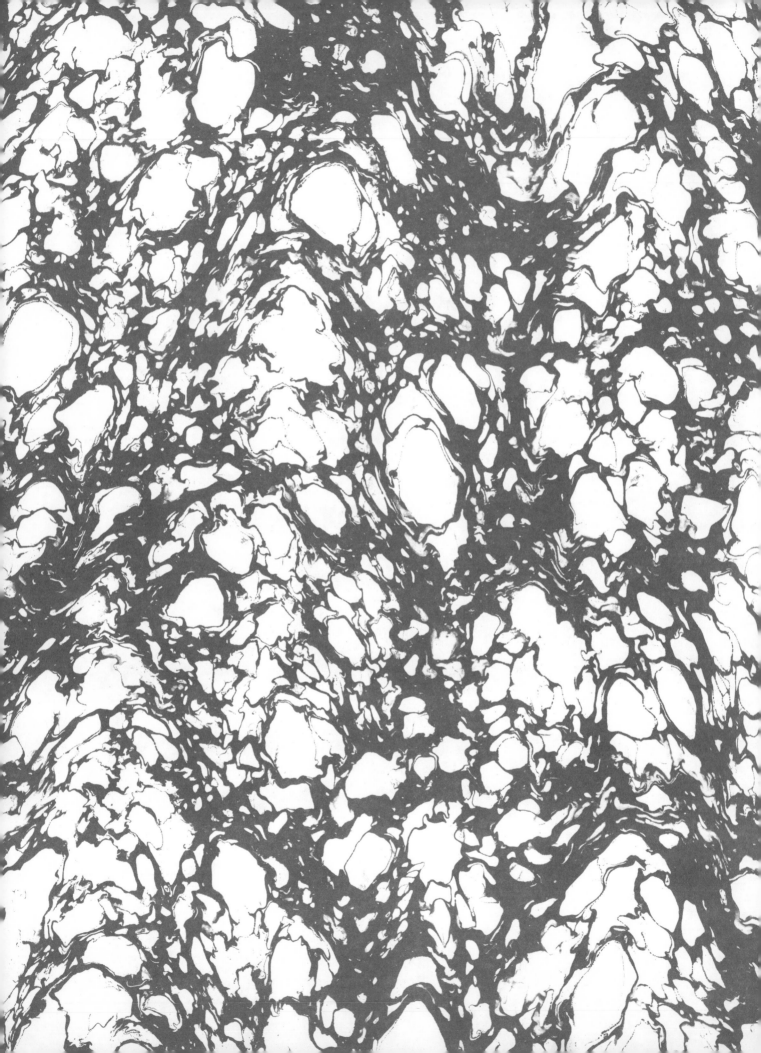